"Trying to figure out how to use social media for more than just expressing how honored you are to have published something? Want to reach other scholars with deeper insights and connect on ideas? If so, this book is for you."

Anita McGahan, *George E. Connell Professor, University of Toronto, Canada, and former President of the Academy of Management*

"I will return to *Social Media for Research Impact* and read it again and again. It offers a clear and thoughtful synthesis of how social media can serve as a powerful tool to disseminate knowledge in academia. I only wish I had encountered it earlier in my career."

Nermin Ghith, *Research Fellow, Charite CCGH / WHO hub for pandemic and epidemic intelligence, Germany*

"This book reframes social media from a distraction into a vital tool for research dissemination, beautifully illustrating how to unlock the full potential of scholarly work."

Yat Ming Ooi, *Senior Lecturer, University of Auckland, New Zealand, and Editor-in-Chief of Research-Technology Management*

"For scholars in non-English-speaking regions, this unique book offers a timely and balanced guide to communicating research beyond English-language journals. It shows how social media can help reach local communities, share insights in local languages, and create real societal impact despite ranking pressures."

Yuosre Badir, *Dean, School of Management, Asian Institute of Technology, Thailand*

"A much-needed guide for researchers who aim to reach a wider community and co-create value through social media."

Oumaima Elbouzidi, *PhD Researcher, Cadi Ayyad University, Morocco*

"This book is amazing as we need to think much more about this topic!"

Aurora Zen, *Associate Professor, Universidade Federal do Rio Grande do Sul, Brazil*

"A clear, practical roadmap for researchers who want to bridge the gap between science and the public and build real impact beyond the academy. Essential reading for current and emerging scholars."

Saud Alomairah, *Postdoctoral Fellow, Johns Hopkins Bloomberg School of Public Health, United States*

"Well-written, thoughtful, and genuinely inspiring, this book shows how social media, used with purpose, can deepen scholarship, spark collaboration, and make research matter."

Lise Justesen, *Associate Professor, Copenhagen Business School, Denmark*

"I don't have a playbook, so this book is one that I and many others can use."

Krithika Randhawa, *Associate Professor, University of Sydney, Australia*

"This practical guide helps young researchers build a clear identity and confidence in making their ideas visible to the world."

Liang Mei, *Research Associate Professor, Peking University, China*

"Bogers and Young move beyond visibility and metrics to show how connection, dialogue, and co-creation can make research truly matter. It's essential reading for researchers, research managers, and university leaders."

Corné Schutte, *Vice-dean of Research and Industry Liaison, Stellenbosch University, South Africa*

"This is a vital resource for every doctoral student who wants to see their ideas move from papers to real impact and truly make their research change the world."

Maximiliano Carlomagno, *DBA student, FGV EAESP, and co-founder of Innoscience, Brazil*

SOCIAL MEDIA FOR RESEARCH IMPACT

This book reviews the effects of the professional use of social media on science and scholarship, providing practical tips, tools, and guidelines for platforms, practices, and routines on social media for academics.

Through concise case studies from researchers worldwide, it illustrates the diverse and often unexpected ways social media enhances academic work, from building collaborative networks and expanding audience reach to creating real-world impact. Coverage includes established platforms like LinkedIn and X (formerly Twitter), emerging spaces such as Bluesky, and creative academic applications of platforms like Reddit and WhatsApp. At its core, this guide emphasises intentional engagement over self-promotion, focusing on meaningful communication, community development, and knowledge sharing. It introduces the Researcher's Social Media Compass, a framework to help you align your online activity with your professional aims, values, and resources.

Social Media for Research Impact is of interest to researchers at all career stages, as well as research managers, advisors, and communication professionals who support research visibility and collaboration through social media.

Marcel Bogers is Full Professor of Open and Collaborative Innovation at Eindhoven University of Technology and affiliated with the University of California, Berkeley. His research and teaching focus on innovation management in general and on open innovation and innovation ecosystems in particular, with a strong emphasis on creating real-world impact in industry and policy. He has been a long-time user of social media and has delivered many talks and workshops to help fellow academics use these tools to increase their visibility, build connections, and create impact. Marcel holds a Master's degree in Technology and Society from Eindhoven University of Technology and a PhD in Management of Technology from the École Polytechnique Fédérale de Lausanne. As a hobby, and to stay fit, he likes long-distance running—an activity that, like creating impact through research, reminds him that the road to success often feels more like a marathon than a sprint. He lives in Eindhoven, the Netherlands, with his wife and three sons, though his years living abroad have given him many places that feel like home.

Mike Young is the founder of the Mike Young Academy, which for over a decade has helped scholars increase their research visibility and supported universities in building networks for lasting impact. He has worked with researchers, research groups, and institutions across Europe to rethink how social media can be used to explore new ideas and foster collaboration. His workshops span a wide range—from low-effort daily routines to long-term influence strategies on platforms such as LinkedIn, X, and Bluesky. Mike holds a Master's degree in the History of Ideas from Aarhus University. In his free time, he enjoys reading philosophy and history. He's also an avid cross-country mountain biker—an activity that, like good dialogue on social media, often leads to unexpected places and people. He lives in Hillerød, Denmark, with his wife and their two children. His adult daughter lives nearby.

SOCIAL MEDIA FOR RESEARCH IMPACT

How Scholars Can Share Ideas, Build Networks, and Make a Difference

Marcel Bogers and Mike Young

Routledge
Taylor & Francis Group

LONDON AND NEW YORK

Designed cover image: Getty Images

First published 2026
by Routledge
4 Park Square, Milton Park, Abingdon, Oxon OX14 4RN

and by Routledge
605 Third Avenue, New York, NY 10158

Routledge is an imprint of the Taylor & Francis Group, an informa business

© 2026 Marcel Bogers and Mike Young

British Library Cataloguing-in-Publication Data
A catalogue record for this book is available from the British Library

ISBN: 978-1-032-96404-1 (hbk)
ISBN: 978-1-032-96407-2 (pbk)
ISBN: 978-1-003-58934-1 (ebk)

DOI: 10.4324/9781003589341

Typeset in Sabon
by Deanta Global Publishing Services, Chennai, India

Declaration of Authorship and Tool Use

All the text has been written by us, the authors, and we take full responsibility for every single word. We used ChatGPT 4o and Claude Sonnet 4 as creative partners in the ideation stages of writing this book. We used transcription software to transcribe interviews, and our own custom-designed GPT on ChatGPT to organise and search within this interview material.

CONTENTS

FIGURES

TABLES

BOXES

PREFACE

Researchers live in two parallel worlds. One is the slow world of peer-reviewed journals, conferences, and formal recognition. The other is the fast world of social media posts, comments, and followers. The former is structured, deliberate, and largely inward-facing. The latter is unpredictable and noisy—but also full of potential for broader societal relevance.

This book is about learning to move between these two worlds with purpose.

Social Media for Research Impact won't teach you how to build a personal brand or game social media algorithms. Instead, it offers a practical and ethical guide to using social media: not just to share your research, but also to connect, ideate, and co-create—and to stay open to the unexpected.

At a time when science is increasingly expected to interact with the wider world, social media offers both opportunities and risks. Drawing on our experience supporting thousands of scholars—through workshops, coaching, and interdisciplinary projects—we explore how small, everyday choices can contribute to meaningful change.

The book combines practical strategies, illustrative examples, and insights from both established theories and emerging research. We advocate a reflective, balanced approach to social media—grounded in generosity, vulnerability, and intentionality.

All chapters were co-written and revised by both of us, reflecting a shared perspective. But they are also shaped by the voices of researchers we've learned from—in conversations, interviews, workshops, and other collaborative experiments over many years. Their insights, questions, and lived experiences shaped the book as much as our own.

In this book, you'll meet researchers who sparked collaborations in WhatsApp threads, used X and Bluesky as real-time learning spaces, and shifted policy debates through LinkedIn. You'll learn why weak ties matter more than you may think—and how your digital presence can amplify your scholarly impact in unexpected ways.

Whether you're just curious, deeply sceptical, or already actively using social media, this book will meet you where you are. It's here to help you build not just a social media strategy, but a strategy for making your research count in the world.

ACKNOWLEDGEMENTS

Marcel was first invited—many years ago actually—by Terry Clague at Routledge to write about his experiences with social media in management research. Nothing came of it at the time—but now, with Mike's involvement and a broader focus on research impact, the time was right. We thank Terry for his persistence, and we appreciate his work—along with that of Naomi Round Cahalin, Laura Slater, and the wider Routledge team—in getting this book into the world.

This book is, fittingly, the product of serendipity—a theme we return to throughout. In 2019, Mike began experimenting with something he called the TwiLi Index, a ranking of Nordic scientists on social media (based on Twitter and LinkedIn followers). One of the most followed names on that list happened to be Marcel, who was then at the University of Copenhagen. That moment sparked the collaboration that led to this book.

Our thinking has since been shaped by many conversations and by generous insights from others. We are grateful to all the researchers interviewed for this book—some featured in case boxes, others unnamed but no less influential. As such, we thank Adam Zable, Aleksi Aaltonen, Anne Radunski, Antonietta Elia, Aurora Zen, Basudeo Dubey, Hannah Chafetz, Ian McCarthy, Jan Recker, Jesper Andersen, Julia Andreasen, Krithika Randhawa, Long Nguyen, Maria Theresa Norn, Marta Stelmaszak Rosa, Pablo Manzano, Rezvan Velayatishokouhi, Sahra Ahmed Koshin, Stefaan Verhulst, Thomas Bandholm, Tony Breu, and Trond Roger Oskars.

Mike would like to thank Lasse Hjorth Madsen, Malene Jensen-Juul, and Hans-Christian Christensen for their early inspiration, as well as the many participants in his social media workshops since 2017 who have contributed with their own practical workarounds and tools—creating a vibrant, evolving learning community.

Marcel is grateful to the many colleagues who inspired him through their use of social media, especially during his time at the University of Southern Denmark and the University of Copenhagen. Now (back) at Eindhoven University of Technology, conversations within the ITEM group—particularly with PhD students and junior faculty—continue to provide energy and insight. Thanks also to the communications department at TU/e, and in particular Marc Rosmalen, for their ongoing support. A special "HT" (hat tip) goes to those who ventured into the world of academic social media early on—including through the workshops in the "early days" at the Academy of Management.

We are both deeply thankful to Christine Møller for her careful editing and insightful suggestions. Her encouraging first impression of the manuscript—calling it "promising"—was a relief and a gift.

We owe much to our families for their patience, encouragement, and support over the past year—especially during the many headphone-filled hours of writing, and for accepting the (free) time we devoted to this "hobby" project. Mike thanks Lea, Atlanta, Benjamin, and Julian; Marcel thanks Hanneke, Lucas, Simon, and Benjamin. (We assume sharing a child's name reflects pure coincidence more than serendipity.) We're also grateful to our parents, without whom none of this would have been possible.

This book is dedicated to all researchers worldwide who pioneer the use of social media in academia—especially those who strive for a well-balanced approach and inspire others by example.

1

INTRODUCTION

Research impact in the age of social media

> Social media became my new way of "walking the factory floor"—
> only now the floor was global.
> —Ian McCarthy, Professor at Simon Fraser
> University and Luiss University

Social media for getting your research out into society

It's the kind of question that surfaces when a doctor finally has a moment to think. Tony Breu wondered why steroids weren't used to treat inflammation of the pancreas. And once he'd plonked himself down on the sofa, the more he read, the more interesting it got.

So, he posted a tutorial on Twitter (now called X)—a thread that unpacked the history of the question, the research behind it, and the possibilities. "We'll do the study", a former colleague and fellow researcher replied. A year later, it had become a reality. A real-world randomised trial had been set off. Not from a grant proposal or a formal collaboration, but from a post on social media.

We'll return to Tony in Chapter 5, and to many other researchers who have had an impact via social media throughout the book. But his story speaks to something wider. As a researcher, it's time for you to rethink how you connect your work to the world. Much of that early-stage curiosity, questioning, and spark can play out in the open spaces of social media. And just like in Tony's case, it needs to speak to real problems and be heard outside the echo chambers of scholarship.

We face multiple societal challenges. Your research can, to some extent, help solve them. But this presupposes that the solutions your research can offer have an influence on people beyond the ivory tower of academia.

Academics are increasingly being asked by universities and funding agencies to demonstrate the impact of their work—impact that goes

DOI: 10.4324/9781003589341-1

beyond traditional metrics like journal citations and academic prestige. Many universities now assess researchers not only on academic output but also on the societal value of their work, using "impact" or "valorisation" (Box 1.1) metrics in their criteria.

BOX 1.1: KEY TERM: VALORISATION

As the EU defines it, "knowledge valorisation is the process of creating social and economic value from knowledge by linking different areas and sectors and transforming data, know-how and research results into sustainable products, services, solutions and knowledge-based policies that benefit society" (European Commission, 2025).

The focus on wider societal impact is also reflected in policy frameworks like the UK's Research Excellence Framework (REF) as well as in the guidelines of various funding schemes. Some universities explicitly reward a focus on outreach or impact through awards, and this is becoming embedded in promotion policies (see Box 1.2 for an example).

BOX 1.2: ALL KINDS OF ACADEMIC TALENT SHOULD COUNT

In 2019, universities of the Netherlands, together with a number of prominent Dutch institutes, published a position paper "Room for everyone's talent: towards a new balance in the recognition and rewards for academics" in which they argue for a broader recognition (and associated reward system) for academic staff. This includes moving away from the number of publications as the main metric to emphasising a broader set of key areas for recognition, appreciation, and promotion. Like in the following:

- Education
- Research
- Impact
- Leadership

This should "enable greater diversity in possible career paths and profiles by recognising and rewarding more diversity in competences and talents" (VSNU et al., 2019).

More important than any awards or promotions, however, is that scholars *want* to make a difference with their work. In our experience, most scholars are not, or not just, doing research to gain citations or promotions. They are doing research because they want their work to have an impact on the world. For these scholars, the professional use of social media is—or should become—a natural part of this endeavour.

This is most likely why *you* are reading this book. Social media can help you bridge the gap between your research and practice, and social media can "translate" your scholarly work into something that is even more relevant to society.

We have written this book for both beginners and experienced academic users of social media. If you are a beginner and new to the professional use of social media, we believe that it will inspire you to get going. If you are already experienced, we believe that the practical tools and cases we include will help you modify, reflect, and improve on your routines.

The book explores how social media can help people find your work and facilitate an exchange of ideas with those people who are beyond your discipline and community. Ultimately, it will help you make a real-world difference. We will not shy away from the challenges and ethical dilemmas involved in using social media. But we will highlight creative, authentic, and generous uses of social media in an academic context. For most professional academic users, this positive use of social media is fortunately the norm and not the exception.

We want to go beyond just giving you a toolkit. We want to offer you a mindset. You could call this mindset the "open academic" (McCarthy & Bogers, 2023). This book is both a call for taking on this mindset and a practical guide to embracing academic openness in the age of social media.

Social media as boundary-spanning technologies

For those with an "open academic" mindset, social media are not only communication tools, but also boundary-spanning technologies (McCarthy & Bogers, 2023). They allow you to extend beyond and cross the boundaries of our own discipline and institution. They let you not only link up and have conversations with researchers outside your field but also with practitioners, policymakers, journalists, students, and citizens. We want this book to enable scholars to become more open, more responsive, more attentive, and ultimately more impactful. See Box 1.3 for one such experience.

BOX 1.3: USING SOCIAL MEDIA TO SPAN BOUNDARIES

What do you do when your work in academia moves you away from the very people your research is meant to help? For management researcher *Ian McCarthy, Professor at Simon Fraser University and Luiss University,* social media became a way to stay close to the factory floor—even after leaving it behind.

A long-time user of social media, when Ian moved from engineering into business academia, he suddenly missed those conversations with practitioners, which had initially made his research more relevant and impactful. "I used to spend 20 per cent of my time walking around factories, looking at plants, and working with engineers", he recalls. "Now I hardly ever spend my time in this industrial reality".

Social media offered an unexpected opportunity to replace some of these real-world interactions. "Twitter [now X] and LinkedIn became my new way of 'walking the factory floor'—only now the floor was global. It was a way to see what non-academics were doing, and actually also what academics were doing".

Platforms may shift, Ian says, but the need to span boundaries and seek inspiration from the people who work in industry will remain just as strong—it is just a matter of adapting accordingly.

We hope to inspire you to become (even) more enthusiastic about using social media for more research impact. This may get you to rethink your overall communication strategy. It may allow you to exchange ideas with decision-makers and those who can benefit from your research. Perhaps—and this is our hope—it will inspire you to rethink and revitalise your entire ambition as an academic.

We see social media as dynamic tools for shaping research impact. But they are still not used enough, and they are not used in a way that fulfils their potential. Social media cannot, and should not, replace traditional peer-reviewed scholarship. But they can broaden how, where, and with whom you share and co-create knowledge. In this way, our view on social media is especially relevant in the context of "open science" (Fecher & Friesike, 2014; Voytek, 2017) and "engaged scholarship" (see Box 1.4), where impact is not just a result of the work, but a way of working.

BOX 1.4: KEY TERM: ENGAGED SCHOLARSHIP

Engaged scholarship is a collaborative form of inquiry that bridges academic research and real-world practice. According to Van de Ven (2007), it involves "a participative form of research for obtaining the different perspectives of key stakeholders (researchers, users, clients, sponsors, and practitioners) in studying complex problems". Rather than separating knowledge creation from application, engaged scholarship aims to co-produce knowledge that is both rigorous and relevant.

Building on this foundation, Hoffman (2021) emphasises that engaged scholars take on the role of active participants in societal challenges, striving to connect their research to broader social and environmental goals. This orientation calls for humility, dialogue, and a commitment to mutual learning between academia and society.

Social media for researchers should be about "purposeful openness". In management research, open innovation refers to how knowledge flows across organisational boundaries in line with a business model (Chesbrough & Bogers, 2014). Just like this, "purposeful openness" for researchers should not be social media exposure for its own sake, with success measured in clicks, profile visits, follower numbers, and reads. Purposeful openness should be a commitment to learning, to collaboration, and to research impact.

As we will see, openness on social media is not always easy. It requires time, reflection, and a willingness to share before everything is perfect. But it is also rewarding. By becoming part of the wider conversation, you can not only increase your individual impact but also help shift the culture of research itself towards more responsiveness, more relevance, and more real-world value. We live in troubled times, and one of the purposes of academic research is to help us make sense of it all. We believe that social media can help increase the impact and legitimacy of academic research and thereby help academic research help the world!

Overview of the book

This book is structured to guide you through the full spectrum of using social media for research impact—starting with foundational concepts and moving through practical steps, challenges, and future directions. After this introduction, we will discuss some of the foundations of social media for research impact. Chapter 2 sets the theoretical groundwork, exploring how social media relate to research impact and academic openness. Chapter 3 maps out the key platforms that academics use today, from LinkedIn to X, through Bluesky, Mastodon, and others, helping you choose the right tools for your purpose. Chapter 4 focuses on building a strong digital identity through professional social media profiles—your academic "first impression" online.

We then move to the more practical strategies that researchers can use. Chapter 5 explores how you can craft posts that create value, translate complex ideas, and generate visibility and interaction. Chapter 6 shows you how to organise your social media experience to minimise distraction and maximise your learning and dialogue. Chapter 7 deals with productivity tools, artificial intelligence (AI), and automation, helping you maintain a meaningful online presence without being overwhelmed.

We then explore other aspects of social media for research impact. Chapter 8 addresses how to navigate the darker sides of social media: conflict, trolling, and misinformation. Chapter 9 shows how kindness, generosity, and ethical actions on social media can help to reinforce a wider scientific community ethic.

Chapter 10 develops a practical framework—the *Researcher's Social Media Compass*—to help you develop effective social media strategies. Then, finally, in Chapter 11, we conclude by reviewing the implications of this approach for university institutions—and the wider ecosystem—and how you can balance the inevitable trade-offs in your own social media activity.

Throughout the book, we draw on both empirical research and practical experience to provide actionable guidance for researchers seeking to enhance their social media presence. We acknowledge that approaches will necessarily vary based on discipline, career stage, institutional context, and personal preferences. Rather than prescribing a single "correct" approach, we offer a flexible framework that researchers can adapt to their unique circumstances and goals.

We offer many examples from research practice, concrete strategies, and critical reflections. This isn't a manual for "just tweeting more", but an invitation to think differently about how you can extend the impact of your work—ethically, effectively, and creatively.

2

BACKGROUND

Research impact in the social media age

> Don't hide in the dark.
>
> —Rezvan Velayatishokouhi, Assistant
> Professor at EM Normandie

Social media and the move out of the ivory tower

For much of modern academic history, scholars have been encouraged to produce knowledge within the confines of their disciplines, often primarily exchanging ideas with their peers through academic journals and conferences. The metaphor of the "ivory tower" reflects this isolation of academia from the real-world contexts where the research could be applied (Etzkowitz et al., 2000; Mowery et al., 2004). The digital revolution—and more specifically, the rise of social media—has fundamentally disrupted this paradigm. And this disruption comes at the same time as other trends have encroached upon the isolation of academia. The increasing importance of university-industry collaboration and the move toward the "entrepreneurial university" (Guerrero & Urbano, 2012; Klofsten et al., 2019, 2024) has led to scholars being encouraged to be more open towards outside inspiration and collaboration. And this ties in well with what social media platforms do as boundary-spanning technologies (see Chapter 1).

Social media are powerful tools for exchanging ideas with colleagues and with professionals beyond traditional academic circles. They enable you to reach a wider audience and overcome the restriction of publishing behind paywalls. As a researcher, you can share your work widely, collaborate within and across disciplines, and contribute to a wider public discourse with a broader group of people who have a stake in your research. And even though there may be differences depending on your situation, including the stage of your career, we believe there are good opportunities for everyone—including (or maybe especially) for PhD students (see also Box 2.1).

DOI: 10.4324/9781003589341-2

BOX 2.1: DON'T HIDE IN THE DARK

If you are just starting your research career, it can be daunting to take part in your field's social media conversation. But sometimes you just have to put yourself out there, according to *Rezvan Velayatishokouhi*, a recent PhD in business and now *Assistant Professor at EM Normandie.* "I tell PhD students: don't hide in the dark", she says "You can't wait in silence for people to notice you. You have to be the one to start the conversation".

But how do you even start that conversation when you're just beginning your academic journey? When Rezvan herself started her PhD, she did not yet have publications or a high-profile project to share. What she did have was the courage to share her curiosity in public. "If I read an interesting paper, I said something about it. I reflected. I asked a question. That was already 'content'".

This slowly helped her build an authentic presence online. "It's not about posting every day or being in the spotlight. It's about being visible in a way that is meaningful. Even a small, thoughtful post can make someone remember you".

Rezvan notes that her willingness to be vulnerable played a big role in shaping her voice. "You can share what inspired you, but also what you struggled with. That kind of openness helps others relate to you—and it builds a more honest kind of community, which you help to shape yourself".

Coming from Iran, social media platforms were Rezvan's entry point to a European academic environment. "It was like a magic passport. Suddenly, I could talk to scholars I'd only ever cited. They responded, supported, and shared their views. That would have been unthinkable without social media".

She has found genuine support and connection on the platforms—from job interview advice to solidarity during challenging periods, she says:

"Finding your voice is not about being impressive. It's about being present—and being real".

Social media platforms serve as boundary-spanning technologies (McCarthy & Bogers, 2023) that enable a new kind of academic openness, connecting you with other scholars, policymakers, industry professionals, and the general public. In line with Chandler and Munday (2016), we understand social media broadly as:

the online and mobile technologies or platforms people use to interact and share content, including social networking sites, social bookmarking and social news sites, geosocial networking sites, blogs, online forums, file-sharing and media-sharing sites, social gaming sites, social commerce sites, virtual worlds, and wikis.

In Chapter 3, we will explore some specific social media platforms that are particularly useful in a research context. This chapter explores the role of social media in facilitating research impact, framing impact not only as dissemination but also as networking, ideation, and co-creation. We will discuss how you can leverage social media to move beyond your own ivory tower and integrate your work into broader societal conversations.

Defining research impact

Let us take a step back and explore what we mean by impact.

Research impact has traditionally been synonymous with impact *within* academia and has been measured by academic metrics like journal citations, h-index scores (see Box 2.2), and grant funding. A more expansive view, however, acknowledges the broader influence that research can have *outside* academia on policy, industry, and society at large.

BOX 2.2: KEY TERM: H-INDEX

The h-index, introduced by physicist Jorge E. Hirsch (2005), has become one of the most widely used metrics for evaluating researchers' productivity and impact in a narrow sense within academia. A researcher has an h-index of h if they have published h papers that have each been cited at least h times. The metric balances productivity (number of papers) with impact (citations), and discounts both rarely cited papers and individual highly cited outliers. The h-index, however, has significant limitations. It varies widely across disciplines, disadvantages early-career researchers, cannot decrease over time, and is insensitive to career breaks (see, e.g., Harzing & Alakangas, 2016 for further discussion and evidence).

We adopt this expansive view of research impact by referring not only to impact within academia but to societal impact as well. This is in line with governing and funding institutions' increased focus on turning research into real-world solutions. See Box 1.1 for broader definition of "knowledge valorisation" to include societal impact. Taking this expansive view, social media provide a significant opportunity for you to increase the impact of your research. They are part of a broader set of communication channels that complement—and sometimes replace—more traditional channels (Bogers, 2021).

In the digital age, disseminating research through journals and conferences remains important, even as the scope, presence, and format of journals and conferences are changing. Social media do nevertheless play an increasingly important role in making you visible and creating other opportunities for impact, such as communicating your research findings beyond academia, getting real-time peer feedback on emerging ideas and concepts, coming up with ideas with practitioners and policymakers, and shaping public discourse on pressing global challenges.

Social media ultimately simply provide a space to "see and be seen" (Bogers, 2021), where you not only share insights but also listen and learn from diverse perspectives. This reciprocal, dialogical nature of social media use is central to maximising research impact.

Why scholars use social media

Scientists use social media in a professional context because of the *functions* they embed. In our conception, also based on Young (2024b), social media fulfil four overarching functions for academics:

- Dissemination
- Networking
- Ideation
- Co-creation

Throughout the book, we will use these four functions as the framework for interpreting how you, as an academic, should use social media platforms for greater research impact. They are summarised in Table 2.1 as the "Reflective Model of Scientists' Social Media Use".

We will have more to say about this table throughout the book—specifically in Chapter 9. But for now, we can focus on the first row, which summarises the strategic or functional reasons for scientists' social media use.

In our experience, academics move to the right in the table as they gain platform experience. They use social media platforms first to disseminate, then to network, then to ideate, and then to co-create. In

TABLE 2.1 Reflective Model of Scientists' Social Media Use

	To Disseminate	*To Network*	*To Ideate*	*To Co-create*
Strategic reasons for social media use	Share your ongoing work with peers, other domain experts, stakeholders, and the wider public	Get access to opportunities, improve your status, meet new collaborators	Get inspired by others' methods Start communities of interpretation Test the scope of your own ideas Manage information	Crowdsource ideas or resources Create collaborative knowledge Invite interpretation from outside your field
Mindful practice	Beware of competing for attention	Seek real connections, not just follower numbers	Allow space for your own deep thought	Be open to loss of control Listen more than speak
Ethical grounds	Be grateful Be truthful (no clickbait) Avoid distracting Be kind (no bragging) Respect privacy	Forge connections between others Attribute and tag Help early career researchers	Contribute *your* ideas to the scientific community Cultivate diverse perspectives Share ideas with colleagues Encourage interdisciplinarity Learn and grow	Trust others' contributions Nurture collective curiosity Leave space for the radically new to appear Disclose your vulnerability

Maturity and experience pathway →

Table 2.1, this is represented by the "maturity pathway" arrow at the bottom.

Let's now look at each of these four functions in detail.

Dissemination—letting others see your work

As a scientist, you can use social media to let your ongoing work and processes, and your finished research findings, be seen by others. By posting on social media (see Chapter 5), you disclose your working self to your peers, meaning your fellow academics both in and outside your own field.

You also make yourself visible to your "stakeholders". We define these as all the people who work with things that have some close relation or association with your research. It could be people working for a funding agency that might sponsor your research. It could be people at your university, working for a lobby group, or a politician's spokesperson in a related policy area. Your stakeholders could also be called your "impact interface" (Bastow et al., 2014), meaning all the non-scientists who, even in some small way, will be impacted by your work.

Finally, by posting on social media, you make your work visible to the general public, in our context meaning anyone outside your peers and your immediate stakeholders—in effect, anyone who is just interested in your work for its own sake.

Networking—meeting scholars and stakeholders

As a scientist, you can also use social media to network with others. You can, of course, network and meet new people *without* social media. But social media platforms let you strategically focus your networking pathways and, in a different way than in real life, deliberately select other new people whom you would like to meet. They also allow you to subsequently validate or confirm—via a "like", "connection", or a "follow"—your in-person, real-life meetings, thereby increasing the chance of future interactions.

Ideation—improving your research quality

As a scientist, you can use social media to improve the quality of your own and others' research by joining your peers in a scientific conversation.

By using social media in this way, you are, metaphorically speaking, uploading and downloading your own thought processes to and from an emergent scientific "cloud"—a virtual scientific public sphere that represents your network of peers. Sometimes you are inspired by others' methods; sometimes you yourself are the source of inspiration. Via your posts, you shape scientific communities of interpretation around the words and images in your post. Social media platforms can in this way help your own scientific thought process. Your motivation to do this is to be inspired by your colleagues within your own specific field.

Co-creation—making something new together

Finally, as a scientist, you can use social media to create collaborative work that goes beyond your own individual inspiration. Here, social media can be a means of crowdsourcing ideas or data. This could be via an on-platform poll of scientists, or links to off-platform questionnaires, or it could be via a virtual live-audio meeting. In this way, social media platforms can themselves be where collaboration and research take place, where the on-platform conversation is not a means but an end in itself. Social media can, in this way, help you invite an outside interpretation that you and others did not foresee, by creating a space for the unexpected and the radically new.

Social media as a tool to link scholars to society

In our conception above, you can use social media to disseminate, network, ideate, and co-create. You can do this with other academics, and this is clearly one of their benefits. But social media also have an impact beyond the academic realm. This ties in with the concept of "academic openness", meaning "a research orientation that leverages insights and expertise from different academic and non-academic stakeholders to co-design, co-produce, and co-assess research that advances academic inquiry and impact". (McCarthy & Bogers, 2023: 154). This definition of academic openness embraces engaged scholarship (Van de Ven, 2007) without sacrificing rigour for relevance. As McCarthy and Bogers (2023: 154) continue:

> Openness is about carefully advancing an academic field without being so immersed that we do not achieve our goal of expanding knowledge that benefits society (Hoffman, 2021). It promotes knowledge flows among individuals within and across organizations and across disciplinary boundaries (see Beck et al., 2022; Bogers et al., 2017; Chesbrough & Bogers, 2014).

Sharma and Bansal (2023) offer an example of academic openness in their study of the mutual knowledge flows between researcher and manager that frame research on business sustainability. They argue that for better impact, researchers need to conduct research with practitioners.

In accordance with McCarthy and Bogers (2023), social media help foster academic openness by doing the following in terms of our disseminating, networking, ideating, and co-creating model: Social media let you share research findings in accessible formats. They connect scholars to policymakers, industry professionals, and the public. They allow you to use social interactions to shape relevant research questions. They use the digital platforms themselves as sources of data and collaborative enquiry. By leveraging these activities on social media, you can increase both the academic and practical impact of your work, making your research more relevant and actionable in the real world.

Measuring research impact through social media

In our expansive view of research impact, it is not enough for you to focus solely on your impact within your own academic circle. Your research can have a broader impact on policy, industry, and society at large.

This has repercussions for how this impact is measured. Traditional academic metrics like journal citations, h-index scores (see Box 2.2), and grant funding will capture only a narrow part of your influence.

As a partial solution to this problem, alternative metrics—known as altmetrics (see Box 2.3)—have emerged to complement traditional measures by capturing online attention to research outputs.

BOX 2.3: ALTMETRICS

Altmetrics—or alternative metrics—are ways to track the online attention that research receives beyond traditional bibliometric scores based on journal citations. They can include social media mentions, news story mentions, blogs, bookmarks on reference managers, and citations in policy documents, and are an attempt to offer a broader picture of how research circulates, both in academia and in the wider public sphere.

Tools like Altmetric.com and PlumX aggregate and display these mentions, providing a more comprehensive picture of how research spreads beyond academic citations (Priem et al., 2010). A study, for example, might have modest citation numbers but significant policy impact or public discussion. Traditional metrics would miss this, but altmetrics might be able to give a fairer assessment of the study's impact.

By using altmetrics alongside traditional academic metrics, you can gain a more holistic understanding of your work's reach and influence (Bornmann, 2014). However, it is important to recognise that, although altmetrics can be an improvement on traditional metrics in terms of measuring real-world influence, they also have their limitations. There is no way of knowing whether the spread of research online necessarily means that it has had an impact. This also extends to academic impact: Research by Luc et al. (2021) suggests a correlation between social media attention and subsequent citations, though the relationship is complex and varies by field.

Despite these reservations regarding altmetrics, they are still useful to evaluate your digital impact. This will not only let you assess your impact—for example, to help demonstrate your broader reach if you are applying for an academic promotion—but also understand where you are doing well and where you might improve.

We suggest that you get into the following habits:

1. Assess regularly which of your posts attract attention, based on conversations you started or in which you had a meaningful exchange with your intended audience.
2. Use tracking tools like Google Alerts or use altmetric tools to monitor discussions of your work.
3. Take note of who interacts with your research and how those relationships change over time.
4. Record instances in which your research influenced policy decisions, industry practices, or the wider dialogue surrounding your field.

These habits will help you move towards a more meaningful assessment of how your work contributes to knowledge, policy, and practice.

A call for proactive digital scholarship

Social media activity cannot replace rigorous academic research. But these tools can enhance its reach, influence, and relevance. By strategically integrating social media platforms into your professional routines, you can move beyond the ivory tower and make a greater contribution to public discourse, policy, and practice.

As this chapter has demonstrated, research impact is now about more than just citations—it's about connections, conversations, and co-creations. By embracing the principles of academic openness, you can ensure that your work has a lasting and meaningful impact on the world beyond academia.

This potential for increased impact comes with responsibilities. You need to maintain intellectual rigour while translating complex ideas for broader audiences. You need to balance accessibility and oversimplification. And you need to use your presence on social media not merely as a promotional exercise, but as an opportunity for genuine dialogue that enriches research itself.

In the following chapters, we will explore how you can do this. We offer practical strategies for building a social media presence, creating thought-provoking posts, and working closely with people affected by or invested in your research—all with the goal of maximising the societal impact of your scholarly work.

3

PLATFORMS

The social media tools that matter

> When I share something—an event, a collaboration—it's not bragging. It's a way to be seen.
>
> —Aurora Zen, Associate Professor at the
> Federal University of Rio Grande do Sul

Academics now have many platform options

In Chapter 2, we summarised how social media can advance academic inquiry and influence real-world policy. After briefly introducing the recent history of social media for academics, this chapter will look at what a social media platform has to be able to do for it to be useful for scientists and academics, including forging so-called "weak ties" (Granovetter, 1973).

At the time of writing, we have just seen an unprecedented migration of scientists away from Twitter, now called X. This we consider to be representative of a wider trend towards decentralisation that changes the whole ecosystem of social media platforms within science. As an individual scientist, this migration and decentralisation enables—and forces—you to experiment with new strategies.

We see social media platforms as a vital infrastructure within science. But most platforms are themselves run as commercial entities, and they may not only have the interests of the scientific community at heart. The 2022 acquisition of Twitter by Elon Musk reminded academics and university professionals of this, and they reacted with a wholesale rejection and migration away from the platform.

With the demise of "scientific Twitter" as an overarching networking infrastructure, scientific users are now forced to take politics, ethics, and the expected longevity of any new social media platform alternatives into consideration when choosing which platform, or combination of platforms, to use professionally.

DOI: 10.4324/9781003589341-3

Indeed, actively using social media in science is suddenly perceived as more risky: why, after all, you may ask, upload "content" in the form of posts and updates if there is the possibility that it will disappear or be used for other unintended purposes?

We believe that the recent trend of scientists opting for social media that are more decentralised, and that prioritise interactions among smaller, more intimate social groups is partly a reaction to these risks.

We will discuss these issues, and finish off this chapter with a distinction between owned and earned media, and what this distinction implies for academics' choice of platforms and strategy.

A short history of social media for academics

In the late 1990s and early 2000s, academics began adopting blogs as personal online journals to share research insights, commentary, data, and resources. Hosted on their own personal websites or on personal pages on institutional websites, the blogs constituted an interlocking network called the "blogosphere". The network was decentralised and allowed for a multitude of individual voices to contribute to the wider research conversation (Kjellberg, 2014). The blogosphere allowed scholars, for the minor investment in time and effort involved in setting up a blog, to bypass the gatekeepers of news media and traditional journals. Blogging allowed faster and more direct communication with peers, stakeholders, and the general public.

With the emergence of centralised social media platforms like LinkedIn, Facebook, and Twitter (now X) and the science-focused ResearchGate in the late 2000s, an even faster, more interactive communication with peers was made possible. Academics started using the platforms to network with colleagues and to show research findings to wider audiences.

The 2010s were the high point of the *centralised* social media platforms, with scientists in different fields sharing and discussing research, mostly on Twitter, sometimes mediated by combinations of science-related hashtags (see Box 3.1). Academic conferences were starting to be organised as partly, or even purely, online spaces on Twitter (Roos et al., 2020). At the same time, LinkedIn and other social media platforms were used for academic outreach to stakeholder professionals in funding organisations as well as the general public.

BOX 3.1: KEY TERM: HASHTAG

Hashtags, or the "#" symbol, are user-generated tags on posts that enable cross-referencing of content by topic or theme. Invented by a Twitter user in 2007, they have become entrenched across all social media platforms. In academia, they can be combined with other hashtags, thereby further grouping and differentiating research topics. So, while #metabolomics, for example, can be used to find all posts with that particular hashtag, the combination #metabolomics #neurodegenerative will find posts that have both these hashtags, to thereby effectively search for posts on the theme of "metabolomics neurodegenerative". This combining of hashtags makes it easier for those who have set up searches for a specific topic (see Chapter 6).

More academics started microblogging, or continuously publishing, the progress of their research in shorter bite-sized updates on platforms like the former Twitter. The platforms thereby became one of the central places where research was discussed, and a space where communities were built around specific research fields.

But this was also the time when scientists and the general public became more aware of the challenges related to data privacy, algorithm-driven newsfeeds, and the platforms' control over user data.

While the platforms offered convenience and potential reach, this often came at the expense of algorithmic control of what you can see as a user, and of distraction through advertising and the promotion of addictive content on newsfeeds.

2022 was a watershed moment in the academic use of social media. Elon Musk acquired Twitter and rebranded it as X. The changes he introduced, including a new pricing structure, and what was seen as the promotion of his own political standpoint, all helped to set off a large-scale scientific migration away from the platform. X was, however, already losing favour among academics due to concerns over data privacy and its perceived lack of content moderation.

All of this helped a resurgence of interest in decentralised, non-commercial, social networks. Platforms like Mastodon offered so-called *federated* (see Box 3.2) environments, where users can better maintain control over their data and contribute to ongoing discussions in spaces that share tighter platform governance structures.

BOX 3.2: KEY TERM: FEDIVERSE

Imagine if you could post from any social media platform, and all your followers on all the platforms you use could see it. This is the promise of the fediverse, and newer social media platforms like Mastodon and Bluesky are already a part of it. For scientists, this means that you wouldn't have to be on many different apps using different algorithms to see the research paper discussions you care about.

Unlike the big corporate platforms of the early 2000s, you would easily be able to take your content, followers, and identity with you if you switched services.

As we write, the biggest challenge for newer federated platforms is making the onboarding of new users as seamless as on mainstream social media. If you already have a large following on one of the mainstream social media platforms, it takes work to build up the same network on one of the newer alternative platforms.

Another platform, Bluesky, designed to be federated, was deliberately modelled on the older, more scientist-friendly Twitter, with more user control over newsfeeds.

These decentralised networks aim to recreate the open, more user-controlled, internet of the early years and provide an alternative to the centralised and corporate-dominated social media. Decentralised communities also prioritise smaller, more intimate social settings rather than virality and mass communication.

At the time of writing, the development of decentralised platforms is still ongoing. But they tap into a growing desire among academics for greater autonomy and control over how and with whom they should interact online.

The strength of weak ties

In one sense, we argue, the trend for multiple decentralised platforms with more user control over newsfeeds ties in with what academics have wanted from social media all along. In his seminal article *The Strength of Weak Ties*, Mark Granovetter argued that weak ties—acquaintances rather than close friends—are crucial for spreading information and opportunities because they bridge different social networks, providing access to new ideas and resources (Granovetter, 1973).

We argue that in science and academia, your strong ties—your close colleagues, mentors, and lab mates—are valuable to you socially, but are often redundant in terms of inspiration or opportunities (Young, 2018). People who are linked to you via strong ties occupy the same academic circles, read the same academic papers, and attend the same conferences and events. As we will talk more about in Chapter 10, your *strong ties* correspond to what is called your "social graph" in social media.

In contrast, your *weak ties*—the people who are further away and with whom you are only acquainted, but with whom you share a research interest—can give you access to new ideas, opportunities, and ultimately collaborations. Weak ties extend your horizon of acquaintances, giving you access to opportunities that you wouldn't have found on your own. They correspond to what is called your "interest graph" on social media.

The concept of weak ties/interest graph explains why researchers overwhelmingly opted for Twitter and LinkedIn as their platform of choice for networking in the 2010s. These two platforms were particularly effective at fostering weak ties. Unlike Facebook—which at the time was the more popular platform in terms of user numbers outside academia—LinkedIn and Twitter easily let you forge connections to people who have your narrow research interest but who are outside of your social and geographical bubble. And they allowed you to filter a newsfeed so that it only shows you posts that are relevant. At the same time, LinkedIn and the former Twitter functioned as a kind of sorting mechanism for both researchers and their stakeholders in the wider global community. Research-related discussions could take place in real time, and interested parties could find exactly the people they wanted for projects. The popularity of Bluesky and Mastodon as platforms for scientists in recent years is also because they enable weak ties to form based on your interest graph rather than strong ties based on your social graph.

Take a PhD student researching climate change policies, for instance. They may have family and friends, and an immediate network that consists of their supervisor, a few faculty members, and fellow PhD students. By actively participating in discussions on LinkedIn, this PhD student can now reach out to a policy expert in another country, a journalist looking for expert commentary, or an editor scouting for contributors to a new publication. These opportunities are less likely to come from their immediate network.

This illustrates another aspect of weak ties, namely, serendipity (see Box 3.3). Weak ties emerge organically and spontaneously from interactions that do not have the tie as the main purpose of the interaction. A casual exchange over a recent paper on Bluesky might lead to a co-authored article. A comment on someone's LinkedIn post could result in an invitation to speak at a seminar. These interactions are small and often spontaneous, but they can snowball into larger professional opportunities.

BOX 3.3: SERENDIPITY IN SOCIAL MEDIA

Serendipity is when something valuable turns up unexpectedly. All professional social media offer you the hope of serendipity, feeding you unexpected opportunities.

Busch (2024), in a wider organisational context, describes three conditions that distinguish serendipity from mere luck or routine discovery:

- **Surprise**: The outcome is not what you were intentionally searching for.
- **Value**: The discovery turns out to be meaningful, insightful, or useful.
- **Agency**: It's not purely random—you still have to notice, interpret, or act on it.

In Chapter 6, we offer you a number of ways to achieve this agency and actively try to steer the random occurrences of discovery.

Migration and decentralisation

Before 2022, the former Twitter, now X, was one of the dominant players in the scientific social media space, and even had a concept named after it: "Scientific Twitter" connoted the emergent, loosely connected network of scientists, researchers, science communicators, and institutions using Twitter to discuss and share science on the platform.

Scientists only ever made up a small percentage of actual Twitter users. But it was easy for scientific users to avoid being distracted by other content. They could choose to only follow and see the content of other scientists. And they could set up curated feeds that only delivered specific types of research-related content, either via third party apps or via Twitter's formerly free social media management tool Tweetdeck.

Changes to Twitter starting in 2022, and signified by the rebrand to X, made it more difficult for scientists to use it as a professional tool, however. This included X giving more prominence to algorithmically boosted content and advertising on the newsfeed, and forcing users to pay a premium subscription for Tweetdeck, rebranded as X Pro, that was now less useful. Some scientists were also incensed by changes to the platform's moderation policies, which allowed more extreme and polarising content to be more prominent.

All of this led to what has been labelled the academic migration from X (Wang et al., 2024), which has happened in a series of waves, with some academics opting for LinkedIn, others for Mastodon, and still others for Bluesky.

Bluesky is a platform that, by design, harks back to the old days of scientific Twitter, and so it is useful to contrast Bluesky with X.

As a larger, incumbent, platform X has a large number of users, and scientists were always a small minority there. Scientists, by contrast, have a larger user share of Bluesky. But this platform has a much smaller total user base and has yet to gain popularity among stakeholders that surround the work of scientists, such as policymakers, professionals in related businesses, students, and the general public.

Given the prevalence of network effects (Afuah, 2013), it is challenging to start a viable social media platform. Until a social media platform reaches a certain size, structure, and conduct, the first users will experience it as being non-functional. This disadvantages new platforms.

What makes academia different, however, is that scientists are split into smaller research fields and communities with close contact between the members. They have distinct names like "microbiology", "climate science", or "digital humanities". Scientists are motivated in their choice of social media platform by what other scientists *within the same field* are doing. They want, after all, to keep abreast of their colleagues. Thus, scientists can move community by community to a new platform, with first movers in, for example, "climate science" first gaining prominence, followed by others (Young, 2024a). This ensures a higher chance that there is already an interesting network for each migrating scientist, as it is not the whole scientific community that has to move at the same time to make it viable. This is one of the reasons why platforms like Mastodon and Bluesky may survive as genuine scientific social media platforms, even though their total audience size remains small relative to, say, LinkedIn or X.

That said, the migration of scientists away from X has accelerated a wider trend in science: the fragmentation of a wider, integrated social media space where scientists interact with other scientists, policymakers, and the general public. A migration to smaller platforms that have separate audiences, interests, and purposes involves the risk that scientists only surround themselves with other scientists, and not the outside stakeholders that ensure a wider research impact.

This is a potential loss for science. In the 2010s, there were only a handful of large social media platforms where scientists were professionally active, and so they functioned as a central discourse space for the exchange of ideas within, and across, professions and disciplines.

The fragmentation of the social media space is also a potential loss for society. Policymakers, funding agencies, and the general public may no longer have the same degree of direct access to real-time academic discussion. This would undermine calls for "open science".

Passive listening tool or posting machine?

Some researchers use social media purely as a listening tool—just using their accounts to keep track of what their peers are doing. These researchers will seldom post or comment on the platforms and, at most, give their colleagues' posts a "like". Other researchers use social media purely as a posting machine, only posting links to their own published work, hoping to gain link clicks and readers. We believe that neither the pure listening strategy nor the pure posting strategy is the most impactful way for you to use social media.

Let us look at the first strategy—only using social media passively as a listening tool. We will go into depth with how you can set up social media to filter your information environment and selectively focus your "listening" in Chapter 6. But if you are *only* using social media passively as a listening tool, you are not getting the benefits that come from people being aware of your presence in the public conversation. Nor are you getting the inspiration for your own work that comes from others commenting on your posts.

Now let us look at the second strategy—using social media purely as a posting tool. This will also reduce your potential real impact. In Chapter 5, we will go into depth on how you can create visibility for your research. But just seeking visibility on its own can also be a trap. It can lead to routines where you mistake the map for the territory, thinking that the metrics of social media views that come from your posts can somehow substitute for real conversations and real research ideas.

If you have a large following among the general public, a pure posting strategy might make sense as part of a wider strategy that includes other types of interactions. But for most of us, the best use of social media involves meeting and conversing online with other academics, and other professionals, who are related to our fields.

This entails using social media to listen to other academics (see Chapter 6) in order to find the conversations you want to take part in, to post (see Chapter 5) to let others know what it is that you are specifically working on, and to take part in the conversation in the comment threads underneath other people's posts. Only in this way can you get the most out of your use of the platforms and further develop your own work and ideas.

Different platform cultures

Different social media platforms are used in different professional and personal *social contexts*. Social media platforms offer, in turn, design *affordances* that reinforce their users' practices on the platform. These users, in turn, through their own posts and comments, reinforce the *culture* of the platform.

Take LinkedIn, for example: it is mostly used in a working social *context*, with the platform specifically targeting professionals, with scientists as a subgroup among these professionals. The platform's *affordances* include the option to write longer posts and an algorithm that reinforces the traction of these longer posts by increasing their prominence on newsfeeds. Users have then, knowing this, shaped a *culture* on the platform where they tend to post in a specific way, partly reinforced by what they perceive as others' expectations of what people should do on LinkedIn. All of these factors—context, affordances, and culture on LinkedIn—result in a specific user experience. For academics, this has meant that newsfeeds (if unfiltered) will typically be filled with other academics' updates on their positive success stories in terms of published papers and receiving grants. In Chapter 6, we will show you how to avoid this.

At the other extreme, Bluesky—much like the former Twitter—is used in multiple *contexts*, not just work, and has everyone as a target user. It is designed as a microblogging platform for continuous updates, and the character limit makes it more difficult to create longer posts (without creating threads, see Chapter 5). Just like the former Twitter, the platform reinforces a practice of continual publishing through its *affordances*, with short updates and pictures of ongoing projects, interspersed with comments on world affairs. This is reinforced by the *culture* on the platform. For academics, for example, a typical Bluesky post could be only one or two sentences and a link to a just-published study.

Sometimes, there is a conflict between the affordances offered by a specific social media platform and the culture of its users. This was the case with the former Twitter when the at-the-time 140-character limit was deemed by some users to be too much of a constraint. The users started posting answers to their own tweets, thereby inadvertently inventing threads and starting a new cultural practice. In academic social media, this led to the writing of tweetorials (see Chapter 5) or tutorials formatted as threads on specific research topics.

The phenomenon of taking up threads and tweetorials in academic social media is a good example of scientists themselves changing social media practices for the better in order to create more impact. Just like the first scientist who made a tweetorial, we believe that you should creatively use the platforms in new ways. The best examples of social media impact come from going past the affordances and routines that are offered and used by others on the platform. You should choose the platforms that suit you personally, but then you should actively and consciously experiment with new formats and concepts.

The advantages of being non-typical

Just as you can consciously experiment with what the mainstream platforms have to offer, you can consciously experiment with non-typical platforms. Marine biologist Trond Roger Oskars (see Box 3.4), for example, has a small-scale, but cumulative, impact on global biodiversity awareness through the medium of the niche social media platform iNaturalist, where he identifies species.

BOX 3.4: SOCIAL MEDIA FIRST, PAPER LATER

Real-world influence can mean deliberately taking action on social media before scientific publication. This is according to marine biologist *Trond Roger Oskars* of the *Møreforsking Institute* in Norway, who discovered cold-water corals in areas previously thought barren off the coast of Norway.

Corals need to be protected for biodiversity reasons, as they function as a kind of "kindergarten" for larvae and as habitats for economically important species. Aquaculture developers need to avoid the corals, as effluent from excess feed can kill them.

Trond and his colleagues faced a choice: wait for peer review or act immediately.

"We went out with a remotely operated vehicle with a camera and checked a fjord. At seven locations with no record on the public map of corals, we found corals in every one of them. We are still trying to publish the scientific paper, but since we are active on LinkedIn and Facebook, people picked up on it", explains Trond Roger Oskars, adding:

"Environmental agencies started calling us: 'Where do we find these corals?'"

This early exposure had a real impact. Conservation discussions gained momentum, and aquaculture developers, who had relied on outdated biodiversity maps, reconsidered site locations.

Outside of Facebook and LinkedIn, Trond has had an impact on global biodiversity awareness through the platform iNaturalist.

"iNaturalist is a sort of social media where people upload images of animals, and experts help identify them", explains the marine biologist. Verified observations then become "research grade" and are uploaded to *the Global Biodiversity Information Facility* (GBIF), aiding conservation efforts. "Through iNaturalist, discoveries are visible almost instantly, benefiting scientists and policymakers".

Another platform that is non-typical, but professionally relevant, for academics, is Reddit (see Box 3.5), where users post anonymously and help to moderate "subreddits" via their upvotes and downvotes. This allows real-world communities of advice to take shape without the barriers of hierarchy or reputation. Scientists can here not only help each other, but also help non-specialists with in-depth expertise.

BOX 3.5: REDDIT: THE CASE FOR ANONYMITY

Reddit is a social media platform built around topic-specific communities (subreddits) where users can post and comment anonymously. Anonymity allows for open and reflective conversations, but this can limit the perceived credibility of the posts and their responses.

The exception is the IAmA (I Am A..., Ask Me Anything) genre of posts on Reddit, where verified scientists and other experts identify themselves to answer questions from anonymous users. The scientist begins the process by starting a post, describing who they are and what they do. Commenters then leave questions and upvote (or downvote) other users' questions that they would like to see answered by the original scientist. Reddit is unique among social media because you don't normally need to prove credentials or identify yourself to contribute. According to *Anne Radunski, PhD researcher at the Hasso Plattner Institute* in Berlin who studies entrepreneurial online networks, helpful insights tend to stand on their own. "Reddit provides so much value. What makes Reddit special is its genuine helpfulness. People share knowledge freely without expecting anything in return—it is community support at its most authentic", she notes, adding that it allows otherwise marginalised voices to be heard. While anonymity precludes fostering professional connections like LinkedIn, Reddit's directness and anonymity create a space for candid insights and real-world advice without the barriers of hierarchy or reputation.

It is good to be non-typical in your choice of platform for another reason. There is a bias in play when you evaluate mainstream (LinkedIn, X) social media platforms' effectiveness. Long-standing and legacy social media platforms typically offer metrics that reinforce the idea that certain routines are impactful. In academia, this leads people to copy typical social media practices from researchers with high follower numbers and likes, reinforcing herd behaviour on the platform, where it seems like everyone posts in the same format. On LinkedIn, for example, you can see "impression" numbers—the number of people who have scrolled past your post—and "engagement" numbers—the number of people who have interacted with your posts in terms of likes or comments. But quite apart from the fact that some of these impressions may be bots and fake users (Binder, 2024), you've got to ask yourself as a scientist: why do I actually need these metrics? The only metric that really counts is your own impact as a scientist. If the purpose of your social media activity, for example, is to find and interact with other individual scientists, then follower numbers, impressions, and engagements may be the wrong metric. If you take them too seriously, they undermine your real impact because you will spread yourself too thin without any real-world payoff.

Non-typical platforms can also be understood as platforms that are designed with other functions in mind, but that have a social media component. Messaging service WhatsApp is a case in point. Box 3.6

describes how WhatsApp has become an effective platform for networking and impact.

BOX 3.6: WHATSAPP ACADEMIA

Messaging services like WhatsApp, Telegram, and Signal are not considered to be social media in a traditional sense, but they take on many of the same functions. While they don't deliberately build public visibility, they are vital for behind-the-scenes networking, planning, and exchange.

For management researcher *Aurora Zen, Associate Professor at the Federal University of Rio Grande do Sul,* the most powerful academic networking tool in her part of the world isn't X or LinkedIn—it's WhatsApp.

"In Brazil and Latin America, WhatsApp is huge", Aurora explains. "When you meet someone, you don't say: 'Add me on LinkedIn.' You say: 'What's your WhatsApp?'"

For Aurora and her colleagues, WhatsApp is deeply embedded in professional life. "I'm in professional groups for the innovation ecosystem in Porto Alegre. It started five years ago with a research project, and now I'm in lasting professional relationships with many people in the city".

Messaging services are not typically oriented towards users broadcasting to all followers like traditional social media, and Aurora's impact happens through messaging in specific closed professional groups. Sometimes her most impactful networking happens in spaces that wouldn't be considered "academic" at all. "People outside academia see my name in the group and say: 'Oh, she's working on that. I'll invite her to this project.' Sometimes they had no idea I existed before".

Sharing updates in these groups serves a broader purpose beyond personal promotion. "When I share something—an event, a collaboration—it's not bragging. It's a way to be seen. To show that the university is active, and we're part of the community", she says.

Aurora's experience highlights how academics' choice of platform can depend on local cultural and professional norms.

For her, the use of the platform blurs the barriers between professional and personal relationships: "Professional connections are often also personal ones. We're open like that. Here, being a nice person is part of being a good collaborator".

In the following pages, in Tables 3.1–3.5, we list a series of social media platforms that are relevant for academics. For each platform, we summarise: who the platforms' relevant users and audience are; key features; examples of current typical practices; suggestions for non-typical practices for your inspiration; our evaluation of their academic networking potential; and the platforms' limitations.

Some researchers prefer to focus on one platform. Others prefer to be active on many social media platforms at the same time. There can be advantages to both strategies. By focusing on *one* platform, you can get to know the culture and features there and easily sustain a routine (see Chapter 7) that allows you to focus on your other work.

But the sum is sometimes greater than the value of its constituent parts—also in social media: using *multiple* platforms allows you to deliberately find and network with other scientists in different audiences and social contexts, using one platform as inspiration for the other.

You can repurpose one post for multiple platforms, knowing that followers on different platforms have little overlap, and even when they do, there is only a small chance of your posts being seen multiple times by the same person. Posts can also be easily re-formatted to the different character limits (see Chapter 7).

Using multiple platforms also lets you become a hub between otherwise separate knowledge networks. Some academics deliberately exploit this with social media cross-posting routines. They monitor one platform for good content in the form of, say, academic papers relevant to their field, then post to their followers on another platform. The strategy is good for the person who does the cross-posting, as they can quickly achieve a following on the platform where they post. It is arguably also good for the original poster of the content as long as due credit is given. The current culture among academics on social media is to give credit by tagging with an "@" sign the person who originally posted the paper that you refer to, thereby letting them know that you have reshared their content.

Owned vs. earned media

The demise of scientific Twitter as a central space for cross-disciplinary debate not only led to many academics opting for alternatives like Bluesky and Mastodon. It has also led to an increasing awareness of the precarity of specific platforms, and to many academics using the platforms' option to download previously shared content.

TABLE 3.1 Mainstream Platforms

Platform Name	Users and Audience	Key Features	Typical Practice	Non-Typical Practice	Peer-to-Peer Networking	Limitations
LinkedIn	Academics, industry professionals, policymakers	Powerful on-platform search field, job postings, option for text and graphic "articles"	Posting links to just-published papers	LinkedIn newsletters functionality for academic blogging, QR code feature at conferences (see Box 4.2)	Oriented towards set-up of professional collaborations	Culture of bragging Newsfeed favours viral content rather than academic posts
Bluesky	Academics, journalists, university institutions	Short microblogging updates modelled on the former Twitter Threads function	Posting links to just-published papers Connecting with scientists in related fields via starter packs	Setting up own starter packs and (public) lists	Strong peer-to-peer interactions and segmented research communities	Non-science audience is politically left of centre

(Continued)

TABLE 3.1 (Continued)

Platform Name	Users and Audience	Key Features	Typical Practice	Non-Typical Practice	Peer-to-Peer Networking	Limitations
X (Twitter)	Journalists, the general public, academics	Well-functioning hashtag culture Oriented towards real-time conversation with other users	Posting research threads Tweetorials (see Box 5.4) Live-tweeting	Polls with tags on the post for quick academic feedback Combining lists and search strings to avoid algorithmically driven newsfeed	Fast, serendipitous connections with journalist and policymakers	Unpredictable platform changes Toxic debates Non-science audience politically right of centre
Mastodon	Tech-focused academics	Federated, customisable networks	Posting research in niche "instances", joining academic-specific servers	Running research group discussions in private instance	Peer-to-peer, but smaller reach Fewer serendipitous encounters	Less discoverability Steep learning curve for new users

(Continued)

TABLE 3.1 (Continued)

Platform Name	Users and Audience	Key Features	Typical Practice	Non-Typical Practice	Peer-to-Peer Networking	Limitations
Reddit	Students, early career researchers, discipline-specific communities	Subreddit communities, upvote/downvote ranking Pseudonymous discussion	Seeking advice in r/AskAcademia or r/PhD, joining field-specific subreddits	Hosting AMA ("Ask Me Anything" threads), sharing research to broader audiences	Strong support communities, but limited personal visibility	Anonymity can lead to harsh feedback Culture varies widely across subreddits
Facebook	General public, university departments, and institutions	Groups Geographically located and well-working "events" function	Student outreach Hosting event pages	Creating private research community groups	Only in closed academic circles	Declining academic use Overwhelmed with AI generated influencer content
YouTube	General public, students, (other) educators	Video content, livestreams, community posts	Hosting lectures, explaining research in accessible ways	Live Q&A sessions, behind-the-scenes lab videos	Interaction with others can be limited on comment threads	Time-consuming content creation Discoverability depends on algorithm

TABLE 3.2 Academic-Focused and Niche Platforms

Platform Name	Users and Audience	Key Features	Typical Practice	Non-Typical Practice	Peer-to-Peer Networking	Limitations
ResearchGate	Academics	Paper sharing	Uploading papers, discussing research in comments	Networking via research Q&A	Built for researcher-to-researcher interaction	Limited engagement outside academia, spammy notifications
Academia.edu	Academics, students	Paper hosting, profile building	Sharing research publications	Using the platform for direct outreach to scholars	More discovery-based than purposeful networking	Paywalls and aggressive premium features
Zooniverse	Citizen scientists, researchers	Crowdsourced research, volunteer participation	Running research projects with public involvement	Collaborating with non-academics on data analysis	Public collaboration with researchers	Limited to specific research fields

(Continued)

TABLE 3.2 (Continued)

Platform Name	Users and Audience	Key Features	Typical Practice	Non-Typical Practice	Peer-to-Peer Networking	Limitations
iNaturalist	Ecologists, biologists, citizen scientists	Species observations, geotagging, identification tools	Documenting biodiversity, collecting data with the public	Using verified observations in research and publications	Facilitates collaboration between researchers and the public	Niche Less useful outside of field biology and ecology
Github	Computational researchers, data scientists, software developers, open science communities	Collaboration on tools, issue tracking	Sharing code, analysis workflows, and data openly for reproducibility and collaboration	Collaborative textbook or syllabus development	Contributions rather than conversations	Primarily useful to those with coding skills or technical workflows

TABLE 3.3 Unconventional Platforms for Creative Academic Use

Platform Name	Users and Audience	Key Features	Typical Practice	Non-typical Practice	Peer-to-Peer Networking	Limitations
Discord	Early-career researchers Students Educators	Voice/video chats, servers, communities	Hosting research discussions, student mentorship	Running informal conference backchannels	Real-time, interactive engagement	Can be overwhelming, requires active moderation
Twitch	Students, science communicators, and curious general audiences	Live streaming, audience chat	Hosting live coding, data analysis	Exploring open workflows	Interactive but audience-driven	Time-intensive, requires audience-building
Pinterest	Educators and science communicators	Visual pinboards, idea curation	Organising research ideas, collecting visuals for presentations	Sharing research posters, infographics	More for inspiration than interaction	Limited interaction, not designed for discussion
Strava	Cyclists, runners, anyone who does outdoor exercise	Activity tracking, social clubs	Non-academic connection to academics in same location	Running/walking meetups at conferences	Common sporting interests lead to connections	Works best for physically active researchers

TABLE 3.4 Direct Messaging and Research Community Backchannels

Platform Name	Users and Audience	Key Features	Typical Practice	Non-Typical Practice	Peer-to-Peer Networking	Limitations
WhatsApp Telegram Signal Slack WeChat (relevant for China)	Academic teams, cross-institution collaborations	Private group messaging, media/file sharing, end-to-end encryption (varies) Localised communities	Coordinating research teams Organising events Keeping in touch during fieldwork or conferences	Distributing job or funding alerts	Used for tight-knit, real-time collaboration and informal networking	Closed platforms—no discoverability or searchability Limited to existing contacts or invites

TABLE 3.5 Other Frequently Used Social Media Channels

Platform Name	Users and Audience	Key Features	Typical Practice	Non-Typical Practice	Peer-to-Peer Networking	Limitations
TikTok	Students, general public, science communication enthusiasts	Short-form video, trending audio, algorithm-driven discovery	Creating short videos explaining research topics, academic life, or teaching tips	Showing lab work, sharing fieldwork experiences, storytelling academic processes	Primarily geared toward public outreach	Limited space for nuance, time-consuming content creation
Instagram	General public, students, science communicators, educators	Visual storytelling through photos, Reels (videos), "Stories" (videos that disappear), and carousels	Sharing images of lab work, fieldwork, conferences, or academic life	Hosting informal Q&As via Stories, building a visual academic brand, using Reels for "explainers"	Limited scholarly discussion or discoverability	Not optimised for in-depth content or linking out to research
Threads	General public, (Instagram users get default account)	Text-first posts, visual integration from Instagram, topic hashtags	Commenting on public issues, sharing broad reflections or links	Experimenting with tone or new science communication formats	Limited academic interaction, not structured for scholarly dialogue	Sparse academic community, unclear platform norms, low visibility for research

Most other platforms give you this option, and it is a good idea to periodically download all of the texts, images, and videos that you have uploaded to a platform (see Chapter 4 for a social media audit routine). The posts, images, and graphs that you have uploaded over the course of years are valuable to you, and you don't want to suddenly lose access to them.

Here, it is useful to bring in a distinction between owned and earned media:

Owned media refers to the content and platforms that an academic has direct control over. This could be a personal blog, the personal page on a university website, or a research repository. But it is also the public-facing profile section of a social media profile (see Chapter 4). This is content and space that you create and manage yourself. Owned media are the digital equivalent of your academic CV—curated, controlled, and designed to showcase your work.

Earned media, on the other hand, are where others share, discuss, or reference your work without your direct control. This includes social media shares by other researchers, mentions in others' blog posts, coverage in academic newsletters, or citations in news articles or other academic papers. Earned media are the digital equivalent of word-of-mouth reputation.

The key is to balance the use of owned media as much as possible for your own research, while leveraging the earned networks that draw people in towards your work, thereby amplifying your impact on your own terms.

Academics have in recent years become increasingly aware of the risks of reliance on earned media. Your uploaded content could disappear or be reformatted to be shown in a different context than was originally intended. But the biggest risk is possibly that the platform where your work is seen loses its relevance.

That said, keeping your original work, images, and data on your *owned* media involves trade-offs in practice. "Earned" dialogue and views of your post on a social media platform are relatively easily achieved. LinkedIn, for example, offers an "article" option that has basic editing tools, a headline, and the option to insert an image, video, slides, links, etc. at the start of each new paragraph. It corresponds to a blog post on your own website. Unlike your own blog post on your own website, which you subsequently have to share to make readers aware of it, when you write an article directly on LinkedIn, it shares that article for you with your connections and the people who follow you. So it is basically like your own blog, but without all the hassle of subsequently having to share the content to make people aware of it.

The downside is that you require your readers to go into the LinkedIn "universe" to read it. When you upload an article to LinkedIn, you are also giving part of the value of the article to LinkedIn, without knowing exactly what it is that you get in return. You are relinquishing part of the "ownership" of this content—making it earned, not owned—and losing at least part of the control over it.

Longevity risk

When choosing a social media platform as an academic, a common concern is whether your investment of time and energy will pay off in the long run. Platforms come and go, and it is not uncommon to see researchers wondering whether a particular network will still be viable in a few years. Some worry about building a presence on a platform that may eventually disappear or lose relevance—raising the question of whether the content they create and share can be reused elsewhere if necessary.

These are important considerations. But focusing solely on the platform's long-term prospects risks overlooking more immediate and personally meaningful questions. A better starting point may be to reflect on whether a platform fits your personal preferences, complements your communication style, and aligns with your professional ambitions. Ask yourself: does it connect me with the kinds of academics and professionals I want to work with? Does it create opportunities to foster real impact for my research?

More fundamentally, it is worth considering whether your use of a platform helps you grow—as a researcher, a communicator, or as a collaborating partner in a joint project. Does using the platform challenge you to clarify your ideas, learn new things, or see your work in a new light? Are you contributing in ways that meaningfully help others? And perhaps most importantly of all: do you enjoy it?

These are the questions that shape a more sustainable and rewarding approach to social media. Rather than trying to predict the future of a particular platform, focus on what it offers you—and what you bring to it—right now. Longevity, in that sense, may be less about the platform and more about your evolving relationship with it.

In the next chapter, we will shift from thinking about platforms to the more practical matter of how you can build and shape your own profile as an academic online—regardless of the platforms you choose.

4

PROFILES

Social media identity for scholars

He had put a QR code to his LinkedIn profile on his lock screen so you could see it without having to open the phone.
—Basudeo Dubey, doctoral researcher at the XLRI - Xavier School of Management

What is a social media profile, and why is it important?

In Chapter 3, we looked at what the different platforms can offer academics. Looking ahead, in the coming chapters, we will look at how you can make effective and valuable posts that are seen by other scientists and stakeholders on social media. And we will look at how you can organise your newsfeed so that you can see the most valuable and interesting posts from others in your network.

But now, we will concentrate on your public-facing user profile. This "public profile" is the part of your user profile that can be seen by other users. It typically includes a profile picture, a cover photo, a piece of text with a biographical description called a "bio", your posts or activity history, and your "connections", "friends", or "followers", depending on the platform's terminology. Figure 4.1 illustrates the different elements of a typical public-facing user profile for a researcher.

Your public profile serves as a snapshot of who you are, and a thumbnail with a link to your public profile will be displayed if someone searches for your name on Google or any of the other search engines.

The public profile is a way to tell other users why they should follow you and is your introduction to your potential audience. Scientists who declare their professional role and identify themselves as scientists on social media are perceived as more qualified and authentic than nonscientist influencers active within their own research field (Zhang & Lu, 2023). Your audiences will identify with and feel a deeper connection to you if you clearly and openly state your speciality and academic

DOI: 10.4324/9781003589341-4

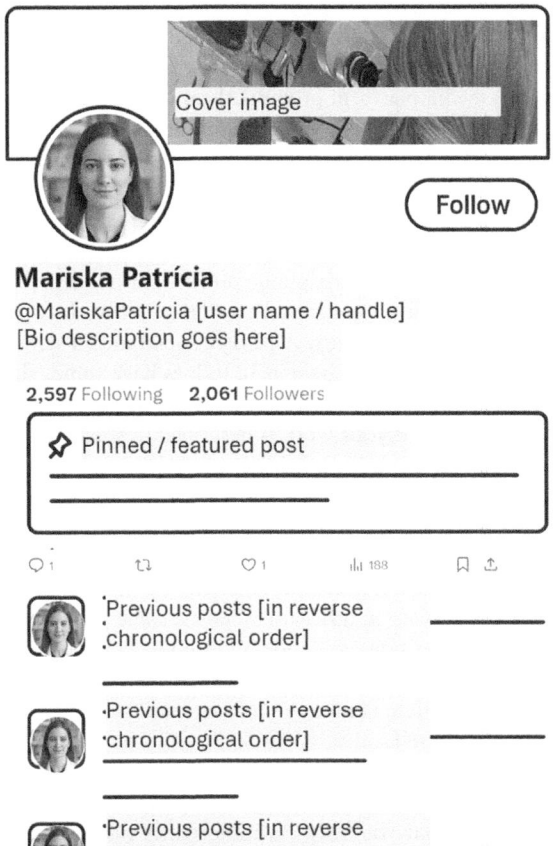

FIGURE 4.1 Typical structure of a public-facing user profile.

Graphic by the authors (fictional profile, face generated by Dall-E).

affiliation. A good public profile will attract other interested academics and stakeholders, who will thereby gain access to your posts on their own newsfeeds (see Chapter 6).

Getting discovered and taking control of your digital identity

Many academics only focus on having a good and up-to-date public profile. They will set up an account on the platform and fill out the sections that the social media platform prompts them to fill out. But then they will only return to the platform to see what others are doing there. They will not post updates or otherwise interact with other users. If you opt to do this, your public profile is the only thing that other users will be able to find if they search for your name, either via a search engine or via the platform itself.

Only setting up an account with a public profile, but not otherwise using the platform functionalities, like posting or interacting, is what is called a *passive social media strategy*. A passive social media strategy is not completely useless (see also Chapter 3). It does have some, albeit limited, value—it lets others find you, especially if you have shared contact information there. And if your work is described in some detail in your profile, it associates you with the field or research project if people come looking for it.

But social media platforms are more useful when you have an *active social media strategy*, and regularly post, comment on others' posts, and interact with others there (see Chapter 5). The reason is that when you post yourself or comment on other users' posts, some users will be interested in learning more about you and will visit your public profile. If they see that you share a common interest, they may opt to follow you (see Chapter 6) or initiate contact either via email or via a direct message on the platform itself.

A typical interaction could take place like this: you have posted a short one-paragraph summary on a social media platform and a link to a just-released paper that you have co-authored. A researcher colleague, "Lisa", from another university, who is following you, sees your post on her newsfeed and reposts it so that it is shown to the people who follow her. A researcher who you don't know, "Leo", but who is using the same methods as you do on another set of data, sees the post that Lisa reposted, and visits your public profile. He realises that you are someone with whom he can exchange ideas and gets in contact with you. You set up a Zoom call and end up working together.

The (fictive) interaction described above illustrates how an activity on a platform, in this case a post, led a user to your public profile. This then led to further interactions and ultimately a valuable co-operation. For Leo, your public profile functioned as validation after he saw your post that had been reposted by Lisa. Your post was interesting, and so he looked at your profile to see if he could find out more before making the effort to reach out to you.

In the case above, it was your post that set off the chain reaction that ultimately led to you interacting with the other researcher, Leo, whom you did not know beforehand.

But even a passive social media strategy can lead to new interactions with your researchers and stakeholders. If you have a well-developed and detailed public profile, other scientists and stakeholders will be able to discover you based on keyword searches either on the platform itself or via a search engine that picks up the keywords on your profile. Being discoverable for a researcher means that other researchers, stakeholders, or colleagues, all of whom potentially could work with you in some capacity in the future, are able to find you.

In our experience, the best public profiles for researchers are ones that are specific in terms of research field, methods, topic, and expertise. The point of having a discoverable profile is not that you get *many* people reaching out to you, but that the *right* people reach out to you, so the more specific and targeted you can be in your public profile, the better.

Public social media profiles are often the first impression that people have of us. This (digital) first impression will often be what others see before they meet us, either in person or at a virtual meeting, and their interpretation of who we are is often shaped by our profile before they get to know us better in a conversation.

This is one of the reasons why our public social media profiles are important. They are part of a larger online "picture" of you that is shown to others in, say, a Google search of your name. By maintaining and managing your social media profiles, you are at the same time mitigating the risks of the rest of your unmanaged online presence. This can include outdated and irrelevant information that can overshadow your current achievements.

Your online presence has its own hidden life, influencing how others perceive you and act with you. Because of this, your public-facing social media profiles help define your professional identity for you and for the people who will be working with you. By proactively working with your publicly facing social media profiles, you are taking control and agency—it is you who defines who you are, not others.

The elements of a researcher's public profile

Later in this chapter, we will offer some specific recommendations for particular social media platforms. But here are some general recommendations that are valid for all the social media platforms that are used professionally by academics. In the context of your professional life as a scientist, your credibility and authenticity are important. For this reason, it is a good idea to strive for consistency across all the platforms where you are professionally active in terms of who you are and what you are doing. This does not necessarily mean that you should have the same profile picture, cover photo, bio, and post the same across all platforms. But it does mean that the profiles that you use professionally should be easily identifiable as you and consistently send the same message in terms of who you are and what you are doing.

Profile picture

If you were to judge by the number of online guides about the subject, your profile *picture* is the most important part of a public-facing user profile. In an academic context, this is actually not the case. A good professional profile picture is nice to have, but the main purpose of it is to confirm that you are who you say you are, and to make you recognisable to the people with whom you will potentially work.

Your profile picture is often displayed as a thumbnail-sized image identifying you next to your posts and comments, and so a picture that is easily recognisable and that makes you seem approachable will increase the chance that people will interact with you.

For this purpose, nearly everyone has a version of the headshot, smiling naturally directly into the camera, and this is actually fine. The best profile photos are ones that make you seem easy to talk to. For this end, a more natural, non-professional-looking photo is often better than a more slick variety taken by a professional photographer. There are also multiple, free AI tools that will enhance a photo taken in a natural context and turn it into a photo that fits into a social media profile format (see Chapter 7 for more on AI tools).

Cover image

Unlike the profile photo, which is also displayed as a thumbnail next to posts and comments, your cover image is only displayed when users go into your public-facing profile. In this sense, it is less important, and some scientists will not use the cover photo at all, preferring to keep the space blank.

We believe that this is an opportunity wasted. Many scientists use the cover image to illustrate their place of work, their methods, or their object of study. As a lab scientist, a cover image could be of your colleagues hard at work looking into microscopes. As a historian, a cover image might be of an ancient manuscript you are studying. As a mathematician, a cover image might be a graphical representation of a mathematical proof.

Often, the cover image illustrates a more light-hearted version of yourself, in contrast to the more serious profile photo. Cover images can also give your profile a more personal angle. They can highlight achievements, messages, or work methods, and serve as a visual tone of voice—expressing the style and personality of the profile.

Bio

Your biographical description, or bio, is the text part of the public-facing profile, and it is more or less prominent on the different platforms. On microblogging platforms like Bluesky, Mastodon, and X, you only have a few hundred characters to work with, and so you need to make it short and sweet. LinkedIn, on the other hand, encourages you to be more wordy, with both a headline and an expanded summary section that can be seen when people click on your profile.

For the platforms with a strict character limit, it is all about focusing on one thing. Take X, for example, with a character limit of 160. Here, most researchers state *what* their field is and *what* they are doing, and add relevant research-related keywords. The idea is to give a visitor to your profile a sense of who you are and what you will post about, so they can decide whether or not they want to follow you.

It can be daunting the first time you have to describe yourself and your work in a pithy sentence for a social media bio. But on the positive side, all the social media platforms make it very easy to edit a bio subsequently, and experienced users constantly update their bios.

In Box 4.1, we have listed a few questions that you can ask yourself before writing this bio. Your bio description could be the response, in one or two sentences, to any of these questions.

BOX 4.1: QUESTIONS TO ASK YOURSELF WHEN WRITING A BIO DESCRIPTION

Expertise: What is your particular *speciality*?
Uniqueness: What *combination* of skills makes you unique?
Access: What do you have *access to* (situation, location, data, people, specialist knowledge) that others don't?
Content: What will you post about?

It is a good idea on a public-facing user profile to "tag" or mention your affiliation in your bio description, as in @ResearchInstitution, where ResearchInstitution is your affiliated institution's own handle on the social media platform. By doing this, you are letting three things happen. First, a visitor to your profile can, on some social media platforms, move their cursor over the tag and see, or visit, the profile of your institution. Second, you are thereby giving credibility to your own voice by associating it with your institution. And third, when other users search for the institution's username in the search field on some platforms, the institution's account will show first, followed by the people who have tagged the institution in their bio. This inadvertently increases the visibility of your profile.

Sometimes you can add a location city. Even though social media are in a virtual space where geography does not matter, there is a higher chance that someone will follow you if they are from the same city, country, or region. However, if you are uncomfortable with adding your geographical location, you will not be penalised.

Your bio is also the place where you can add a link to your institution's website, or your own personal blog, or research repository.

Platform-specific strategies for profiles

LinkedIn

LinkedIn, more than any other social media platform, wants you to fill out your public-facing user profile. While other platforms offer minimalist bio sections, LinkedIn provides what feels like an endless series of boxes to fill out, enabling you to publicly display a complete CV of past achievements and a storyline that builds up to where you are now. Many researchers and other professional users opt to complete all sections, including descriptions of their publications and past affiliations. There is no reason not to fill out as much as you can—but it can be time-consuming. That said, one of the most important elements is your headline with the first words shown after your name. If you don't customise it, LinkedIn will auto-fill it with your current job role that you have filled out in another section. But because the first few words after your name appear alongside your name in all interactions, it's worth crafting this line carefully. Ideally, you would include your field, research object, methodology, or technology within the first few words—this makes you more memorable. But less than this will suffice.

Below the headline, the "About" section gives you 2,600 characters to tell your story. Still, even though LinkedIn offers you ample space, less is more. Further down, there are many sections where you can highlight your experience, projects, and publications—giving visitors a broader view of your professional journey.

The words you choose in your headline and the words you choose to describe yourself in the "About" section also act as keywords that help others find you via LinkedIn's own search engine. So, if your expertise is in "cell biology", using that exact phrase in either place makes it easier for users interested in that topic to discover your profile. We will explore how to actively use keywords to improve your own newsfeed in Chapter 6, but it is helpful to know that searchable keywords make your profile more discoverable to others.

LinkedIn plays a peculiar game of hide and seek. It sends a flood of notifications to its users—though to its credit, most can be turned off. A distinctive one is the alert that someone has viewed your profile. Ironically, this may discourage people from casually visiting profiles, as they'd prefer to browse anonymously, like on other platforms. LinkedIn's premium version allows this anonymous browsing, which is useful, for instance, for recruiters. But for researchers, however, this feature per se may not be sufficient grounds to pay for the premium version. We also believe that it's a good thing to know who has looked at your profile—as it can spark collaboration opportunities by surfacing connections you didn't know yet.

Finally, LinkedIn has a fun and practical feature: a QR code that links directly to your profile. Box 4.2 shows how you can use this at conferences and events to make connecting even easier.

BOX 4.2: THE QR SCREEN TRICK

There are only a few other academics in India working on the exact topic (open innovation) of *Basudeo Dubey, Doctoral Researcher* at the *Xavier School of Management (XLRI)* in Jamshedpur, India. So he has used LinkedIn to find others—and get himself noticed—within his field.

"The problem with my PhD research is that in India there is little focus on 'open innovation', as it's largely a 'Europe-centric' topic for the lack of a better word. So the only way I could enter into the discussions was via social media", says Basudeo. "Going to guest lectures or attending teaching staff classes was just not an option".

He adds that a professor at a European university had mentioned a winter school programme on LinkedIn, saying that those who are interested can reach out to this link and apply. "I wouldn't have been able to get this information via my colleagues or staff, via flyers, or via the library at the college. So I'm entirely dependent on social media to keep track of the activities that are going on", says Basudeo.

He mentions one thing on LinkedIn that others should know about:

"I picked up on this trick last year from someone when I was at a conference in Bilbao, Spain. LinkedIn provides a QR code that leads you directly to your profile and this is great for events. Screenshot your QR code, and put it on your lock screen on your phone so you can see it without having to open the phone via your pincode. When you meet someone at a conference who asks for your contact details, you just show your phone screen, and they can scan and click follow or connect. A frictionless way for people to sign off, and better than messing around with business cards or emails!"

Bluesky

Bluesky belongs to the microblogging group of platforms (see Chapter 3) and has modelled its public-facing user profile on the old Twitter (now X), something that has endeared it to scientists.

Like the other microblogging platforms, it has limited space in its bio section and orients users towards looking at the posts and feeds rather than dwelling on a user's extended profile section. The bio section has only 256 characters available, and so it is all about precisely letting visitors to your profile know why you should be worth following in the first place.

However, there is a workaround to give yourself some more space to let visitors know who you are and what you do. It is the pinned post (see Figure 4.1). Just like on X and Mastodon, and on LinkedIn, where it is called "featured posts", you can pin one of your posts to the top of your profile, so that it is not superseded by your later posts when people are viewing your public-facing user profile.

As a researcher, you could, for example, post an update with a few sentences and links to the project you are currently working on and pin it to the top of your profile. This effectively gives you extra space to present who you are. Then, every time you start work on something new, you pin that post to the top of your profile, and it will then take over the pinned position.

Mastodon

Compared to other microblogging platforms, Mastodon has a bit more to play with in its bio section with 500 characters, and a series of fields that you can fill out with whatever you want. For researchers, these fields should be filled out with links to any personal websites, blogs, your page on your institution's website, or the URL linking to your profile on other social media platforms.

X

The former Twitter has 160 characters to play with in its bio section and makes any links you put in this bio description section inactive. But it has one link option underneath, where you can link to whatever you think is the most important. Watch out, though. Any account handles of directly competing platforms like Bluesky will be made inactive.

That said, if you do use Bluesky or another platform, it is still a good idea to put your account handle of a competing microblogging platform in your X bio for the following reason: since people started to migrate from X to its competitors like Bluesky and Mastodon, a number of third party applications allow you to "bridge" between the platforms, letting you find the people you follow on X, on for example Bluesky. If you are part of someone else's X network and they use a bridging app, the Bluesky account reference in your X bio, even though it is inactive and non-clickable, will make sure that you come up on their list. Bridging is particularly important to those who have already built up large networks on X and need to build a new network on another platform.

Auditing your social media profile presence

We often take it for granted that the people we meet in our professional lives only know us and appreciate us from the real-life interactions that we have with them. But people will look us up digitally before and after we interact with them, effectively making our social media profiles an important first or second impression.

That is why you need to do a regular social media audit. Luckily, it's easy. For all the social media platforms that we analyse in this book, adjusting public-facing user profiles is easy, and you can retrieve an archive of your posts on the platforms. Box 4.3 provides a routine.

BOX 4.3: A ROUTINE FOR AUDITING YOUR SOCIAL MEDIA PROFILE(S)

1. *Google yourself*
Search for your name in Google (in incognito mode) and see what appears. Is there any outdated, incorrect, or irrelevant content from your social media profiles that is displayed on the search results page? Edit your profiles or delete the irrelevant posts. While you are at it, check your Google Scholar, ResearchGate, ORCID, and institutional profiles to confirm accuracy.

2. *Review your social media profiles and bios*
Now look at the public-facing user profiles on the platforms you use. Update them to reflect your current position, research, and interests. Do the profile pictures and cover photos align with your professional identity? If not, change them. Confirm that the contact information and links are there if you have a personal website, Google Scholar, or institutional page.

3. *Assess past content and comments*
Scroll through your past posts and delete or archive anything that you don't think reflects your professional identity.

---

4. *Update publications and professional links*
Make sure all your relevant academic works (publications, conference talks, blog posts) are linked to in your public-facing profiles.

5. *Email signature*
Link to your social media profiles on your email signature. If there is not enough space for all these links, you can set up a Linktree link, which is a free basic landing page for your social media profiles.

6. *Physical business card*
Do you use a physical business card? This is the time to update the links on it.

7. *Privacy and security check*
Now review the privacy settings on all your platforms. What is public vs. what is private? Remove any personal details that you do not wish to be public, like an address or a personal email, for example. You can, if you choose, set up two-factor authentication on your social media accounts.

8. *Set up a recurring audit schedule*
As a final step, set up a calendar reminder to audit your social media profiles again in one year's time.

Apart from this, you can, of course, update your social media profiles whenever you publish a major paper, or if you change job or role, speak at a conference, or receive an award (see Chapter 5).

5

POSTS

Making your research visible

> If I could interview all the people who read my tweetorials ... I bet most people would not remember much. But the main learner is me—anyone else who learns is just gravy.
>
> —Tony Breu, Assistant Professor
> at Harvard Medical School

Translating research into online interactions

In Chapter 4, we focused on public-facing user profiles. However, getting the most out of social media will require more than simply having profiles on various platforms. To connect with others effectively on social media requires the thoughtful translation of your complex research findings into a format that people in your different audiences can use. It requires some strategic planning, and it requires authentic interactions with the people you meet. A well-crafted post can set off conversations and invite collaboration with, and inputs from, people who you do not know yet. Social media communication should be seen as a two-way exchange where you both share your work and listen to others—creating the potential for new collaborations, research opportunities, and real-world impact.

While simply being present on social media is a step in the right direction, the platforms offer many more opportunities to further exchange ideas with others in ways that can enhance your research impact. How you post, comment, and interact on the platforms matters—the tone of your comments, the format of your posts, and the frequency of your posts all influence how your audiences will perceive and interact with you and your research. This chapter will explore strategies for creating post formats that make people stop and read, and that resonate with each of your audiences.

DOI: 10.4324/9781003589341-5

Connecting with others on social platforms

In Chapter 4, we contrasted an active and a passive strategy on social media. *Active* social media usage refers to posting, liking, commenting, and sending direct messages, while *passive* use refers to the monitoring of others without any direct interactions with them (Trifiro & Gerson, 2019; Verduyn et al., 2017).

To sum up, being active on social media means posting regularly, discussing with others, and sharing your own insights in the comments. Being passive on social media sounds like something negative. However, it simply means following relevant accounts, observing trends, scrolling newsfeeds, and clicking on posted links, and potentially learning from the discourse without you yourself offering posts or comments.

Many scientists take a hybrid approach. They post periodically, with spurts of purposeful activity—including commenting on others' posts and participating in discussions—in connection with events, their own milestones, and publication of their own papers.

In Chapter 3, we introduced how the exchange of ideas on social media platforms could be understood through the lens of network theory (Granovetter, 1973). This perspective helps explain how researchers form connections that bridge diverse communities and disciplines. Social media platform use can also be understood through the lens of uses and gratifications theory (Katz et al., 1973). People are motivated to use media to satisfy particular needs—including information seeking, professional identity development, and social connection.

As a researcher on social media, you can adopt different roles in the overall landscape, as proposed by McCarthy and Bogers (2022) and described in Box 5.1.

BOX 5.1: RESEARCHER ROLES ON SOCIAL MEDIA

McCarthy and Bogers (2023) propose four archetypes for researchers using social media:

- **Observer**: Monitoring discussions to gather insights and identify emerging trends.
- **Connector**: Facilitating interactions between individuals and groups to foster collaboration.

- **Promoter**: Sharing and disseminating research findings to a broader audience.
- **Influencer**: Shaping discussions and opinions within specific domains.

By adopting these roles, you can enhance your openness and impact, effectively translating online interactions into real-world applications.

Your own approach and role may evolve over time, depending on your needs, career stage, and available time (see Box 2.1 for a specific consideration for PhD students). The key is to use social media *with intention*. Decide what role you want social media to play in your professional life and adjust accordingly. To reiterate McCarthy and Bogers (2023), researchers can embody different roles on social media, ranging from passive observers to active influencers, each with its own benefits and commitments.

Balancing personal and professional content

A common dilemma for researchers is whether to mix posts that relate to their profession as scientists with posts that refer to their personal or non-academic lives. While some prefer to keep their social media activity strictly professional, others find that sharing personal insights helps humanise their work and build an audience that cares about them.

Those who opt for the first, strictly professional, approach, with a focus solely on research updates, publications, conference insights, and academic discussions, have the advantage that they can effectively partition their research life from their other interests. This allows for a social media "detox" at the end of every working day. Others may prefer the second approach, blending personal and professional experiences, "behind-the-scenes" work, or reflections on academic life.

In our opinion, your decision should *purely* be based on what you are comfortable with. Your audience is used to both types, having people in their network who blend personal and professional posts with those who only post professionally, and will generally welcome your social media activity no matter what.

One way to sidestep the dilemma is an approach adopted by some scientists, namely to segment types of posts into different profiles and accounts, or different platforms, to maintain a separation between their professional and personal lives. Having separate microblogging accounts on platforms like X, Bluesky, and Mastodon is actually very simple, and it has few coordination costs as the platforms deliberately make it easy to switch between your different accounts. Confusion with followers can be avoided by clearly stating in the bio description what the account is used for and referring to your other accounts on the same platform. This strategy allows for a professional profile that is more open to following peers and is research-related, and a personal profile where you maintain more control over who you follow and where the posts are related to your non-professional interests.

In every case, authenticity is a key aspect to keep in mind, regardless of the exact approach you choose. What it's about is *you* sharing your experiences, challenges, and perspectives in a way that aligns with *your* personality and professional goals. This is what will ultimately connect you to your audience.

Fostering real-world conversations

Kietzmann et al. (2011) identify *conversations* as one of the seven functional building blocks of social media, emphasising the importance of dialogue in building relationships and community. Engaging in conversations allows researchers to share insights, get feedback, and co-create knowledge with their audience.

One of the most valuable aspects of social media is its ability to turn the passive consumption of "content", in the form of posts, into active dialogue. Box 5.2 offers some recommendations on how to foster meaningful conversations.

BOX 5.2: CULTIVATING MEANINGFUL DISCUSSIONS

Ask questions: Invite discussion by posing thought-provoking questions related to your research.
Respond to comments: Acknowledge and discuss with those who interact with your posts.
Join trending discussions: Participate in relevant conversations, such as conference hashtags or emerging research debates.
Encourage knowledge exchange: Share open-access articles, highlight interdisciplinary insights, and create spaces for constructive dialogue.

Social media are not traditional media and should not be used as one-way broadcasting tools. Look at them as dynamic spaces where real-world collaborations and the exchange of knowledge can happen.

Translating complex research into accessible posts and visuals

Making research accessible requires tailoring what you share of your underlying work and research to your different audiences. The same findings, explanations, and activities can be shared in multiple formats, each suited to different domains of expertise. Box 5.3 gives a few examples of possible formats you may consider for visualising your research, but there are many others.

BOX 5.3: SELECTED EXAMPLES OF FORMATS FOR VISUALISING YOUR RESEARCH

Threads: A concise, structured narrative, consisting of a series of inter-linked posts, used for breaking down complex findings step-by-step. It can be used on the microblogging platforms.

Infographics and visual abstracts: A way of turning data into visually appealing summaries that enhance comprehension.

Reels and short videos: Format for communicating key concepts in engaging, bite-sized formats.

Carousels: Layering information across multiple slides, where the user clicks right, slide by slide, to see a narrative.

Academic writing is typically structured to prioritise precision and depth over accessibility. Social media posts typically demand a different approach—one that prioritises clarity and brevity without sacrificing accuracy. Social media posts are often read by audiences that have a different domain of expertise than the audience of the academic paper. This means that a "translation" process is needed to democratise the knowledge inherent in the academic paper and expand its impact beyond traditional academic boundaries.

In the above, we put the phrase "translate" in inverted commas. The word implies a hierarchy with the academic paper closer to "original research" than the social media post, which is then somehow derivative. This is not necessarily the case. Take the tweetorial (see Box 5.4), for example, which is a combination of the words tweets and tutorial, which means a thread of posts on X that is structured as an introduction to a specific research question or topic. The discussion that takes place on the tweetorial can be closer to the actual research process than the academic papers to which the thread refers.

BOX 5.4: TWEETORIALS

He didn't set out to change how medical knowledge spreads on social media. He just wanted to explore an interesting question. But the "tweetorials" of *Tony Breu, Assistant Professor at Harvard Medical School*, ended up becoming a template for good science communication in the health sciences and an inspiration to many others.

Tweetorials is a combination of the words tweets and tutorial and means a thread of posts on X that is structured as an introduction to a specific research question or topic.

Tony Breu recalls his first tweetorial in 2018.

"So I had thought about this question in the shower the day before and it was really gnawing at me: Why does someone's hematocrit, the concentration of red blood cells decrease, when they have an acute bleed? When you're bleeding you bleed whole blood, so the concentration of hemoglobin shouldn't change", he recalls.

"I thought, let me sit down at my computer in front of the TV and throw together something with no expectation that anyone was going to be interested. At that point, I had a few hundred followers at most. But if you're able to engender an interest in just a few small parties who have more of a following than you, then it has the ability to explode", he says, adding that it turned out to be the most popular thing he'd ever done. Now, hundreds of tweetorials later, he has a mass following on X and his new account posting the same tweetorials on Bluesky already has a large following there also.

Tweetorials walk readers through a concept step-by-step, much like an academic paper or a mini-lecture. Each of the underlying tweets in the thread can be retweeted, questioned and discussed by other experts. For Tony Breu, they became a way to think through complex questions, engage with research literature, and share insights in an accessible way.

The impact went beyond communication to, and with, an expert audience: one of his tweetorials questioning why corticosteroids were not used for pancreatitis directly inspired a team of researchers to launch a clinical trial on the subject.

Tweetorials serve as a good example of how social media are boundary-spanning technologies (see Chapter 2). In Tony Breu's case, the tweetorials connect different otherwise siloed health research communities with clinical practitioners. Tweetorials allow generalists like Tony Breu to engage deeply with specialists.

Tweetorials take time to set up. With the review of the literature, the downloads, the reading, and the construction of the tweetorials, Tony Breu averages three to five hours for each. But it may still be time well spent.

"Tweetorials" are already being used on newer platforms like Bluesky. And Tony Breu sees them as a rewarding part of his own self-development as a scientist and clinician.

"If I had the ability to interview all the people who had read them, three months after they were posted, I bet you most of those people would not remember much. These topics are complex. But the main learner is me—anyone else who learns is just gravy".

Images, diagrams, illustrations, and videos can dramatically increase the attention your research gets. According to research by Borkin et al. (2013), visualisations that contain recognisable objects and elements like faces and voices, and less "chart junk", are more memorable than abstract visualisations.

Focus on simplicity by conveying one clear message per visual post. Support this clarity with enough context to ensure your audience understands the background and relevance. Aesthetic appeal also plays a crucial role: consistent colours, readable fonts, and well-balanced layouts help maintain interest from your audience. Above all, accuracy is essential—visualisations must represent the underlying data faithfully to maintain credibility.

Some researchers worry that simplifying their work compromises its integrity. However, effective science communication is not about "dumbing down" content but about making it accessible to non-peer audiences without losing the essential meaning. As Olson (2018) notes in his book "Houston, We Have a Narrative", scientific storytelling is about creating narrative connections that help audiences understand complex ideas.

Good science communication is not about simplification. It's about *framing* research in a way that resonates. See Box 5.5 for some possible techniques to consider.

**BOX 5.5: SOME TECHNIQUES FOR
FRAMING YOUR RESEARCH**

Use relatable analogies: Connect abstract concepts to everyday experiences.
Focus on the "why": Explain the significance of the research before diving into the details.
Show real-world impact: Highlight how findings contribute to solving pressing challenges.
Employ narrative structures: Frame research as a journey of discovery, complete with challenges and breakthroughs.

A well-crafted post doesn't just inform, it invites interest, feels real, and encourages a response. This requires understanding not just your research, but also your audience and how they consume information.

From visibility to impact

Maximising research impact on social media is not just about being present but about interacting in a way that aligns with your goals and personality. Social media offer powerful tools to make your research visible and set off meaningful conversations. This goes for actively participating in discussions, sharing carefully curated insights, or using visual storytelling techniques.

The most effective social media strategies for researchers are grounded in a few key principles. Consistency in posting helps build expectations and encourages return visits. Authenticity—sharing honest insights and experiences—helps foster trust. Accessibility implies translating complex research into understandable content to broaden your impact. Finally, reciprocity matters: interacting with others by commenting, sharing, and reacting to their work contributes to a more collaborative and open academic community.

By learning from successful examples and experimenting with different approaches, you can harness social media to create value—not just for your career but for society at large. But to create value, you need to protect your own attention. In the next chapter, we will explore how to organise and manage your social media attention efficiently, ensuring that these platforms enhance rather than detract from your research productivity.

6

CURATION

Using social media to filter your information environment

> Strategic listening like this takes time [...] but over time, your feed
> starts to speak back to you.
> —Maria Theresa Norn, Associate Professor
> at the Technical University of Denmark

Attention: Your key research asset

While our last chapter was about optimising an outgoing activity, posts, this chapter is about optimising an "ingoing" activity, namely, the incoming information that comes to you from social media. By deliberately and consciously tweaking the character of this inflow, you can harvest the gains to your research that come from social media, with the least possible distraction.

This chapter offers a number of ways to give you agency and to actively steer towards less random discovery occurrences (see Box 3.3 on serendipity). The platforms themselves offer numerous solutions, like "save" or "bookmark" buttons on posts. Sometimes scientists find better ways—simply "liking" a post on X or Bluesky is often more practical and lets you return to all the posts that you discovered for later reading. We, however, want to be more systematic. In an ideal world, social media platforms should help researchers stay informed about their own and related research fields; the professions and jobs that they impact, and that impact them; as well as related policies and technologies. However, the social media platforms that are used by scientists are not solely built for scientists, but also for other users who have other interests and priorities. Moreover, the incumbent platforms are commercial. They are paid for, mostly, by showing advertising to potential consumers, and they therefore have an interest in showing content that keeps users glued to newsfeeds. Outside of a science context, researchers are themselves target users and consumers of the platforms. In the same way as other consumers, they will scroll on platforms like X,

DOI: 10.4324/9781003589341-6

Bluesky, Reddit, Instagram, and LinkedIn in non-research contexts, too, for their interest and entertainment during non-working hours.

The current social media platforms used by scientists are not designed within a scientific context. This is not from any ill will on the part of the platforms. Their business model and commercial survival depend on them being designed for, and targeting, an audience in a non-scientific, consumer context.

Some writers decry the exploitation of users of social media platforms through data extraction (Zuboff, 2019). Others contrast a more authentic "deep work" with the distraction of social media users (Newport, 2016). But you could also argue that researchers' professional use of social media "exploits" commercial platforms for public gain in the form of better science.

Indeed, this is what we want to do in this chapter. We will present techniques to "exploit" social media platforms' newsfeeds for your professional gain, without having to "pay" in the form of your distraction and attention.

Research demands sustained concentration. It thrives on deep work, a term popularised by Cal Newport (2016) to describe uninterrupted, focused cognitive effort. Social media apps consciously design their user experience to interrupt this deep work, as they are competing for users in the attention economy, where your time on their apps translates directly into revenue. Social media deliberately try to keep you scrolling and clicking on notifications as a means to this end. Legacy social media also generally want you to personalise one, centralised, newsfeed on their app, so that they can capture as many of your attention minutes as possible.

But without a structured approach to managing your attention, you risk becoming stuck in a cycle of scrolling through feeds at the expense of gaining new research collaborators and developing your own thoughts and work.

This is why we recommend that you set time aside for social media, and this means consciously and strictly *avoiding* social media outside these time slots (see the section "Customising your social feeds"). With this recommendation, we stand in opposition to what the social media platforms themselves, and many of the social media influencers that tend to have prominence on the platforms, recommend to achieve success as they define it. But, we argue, you are not on the platform to achieve success in terms of a platform's own metrics. You are on social media to become a better scholar, to meet the people you want to work with, and to increase the impact of your work.

Following with intention

When you "follow" someone on a social media platform, their posts become part of the default newsfeed you see when you open the app or website. By following someone, you choose what kinds of conversations and ideas will surface on the newsfeed that opens first on the app (see Box 6.1).

In the section "Customising your social feeds", we will get into customising alternatives to this default social media newsfeed. But for now, let's take a look at the default social media newsfeed.

The default newsfeed on any platform is shaped by who you've chosen to follow. Algorithms may amplify or distort this, but the root signal comes from the people you follow.

We recommend that you take a pause before hitting the follow button. Ask yourself: does this person share insights that are relevant to my research or the impact I hope to have? The people you follow should be people you want to learn from.

You might think of your following list in clusters:

- Researchers in your own field
- Interdisciplinary thinkers adjacent to your work
- Policy professionals or practitioners who are relevant to your field
- Journalists who cover your topic area
- Academic institutions or funders

When someone notices that you've followed them—depending on their settings, they may get a notification—they may choose to look at your profile in return. If your profile clearly signals your research focus or professional identity, this can prompt them to follow you back. Your posts may now appear in their feed, and future interactions become more likely. In this way, following someone isn't just a way to listen—it's a subtle invitation to be seen.

Some users treat following as a growth tactic rather than a genuine act of interest. They follow large numbers of accounts hoping for follow-backs—a tactic, often automated or done in bulk, that is common among influencers and marketers. Researchers should approach this tactic with caution, however. In academic contexts, where trust and authenticity matter, following should reflect real curiosity or professional relevance—not a numbers game.

Equally important is the act of unfollowing. It's not considered impolite, and the platforms do not send notifications to users saying that so-and-so unfollowed them. Unfollowing accounts that no longer contribute meaningfully to your research or research impact work is a healthy practice. Unfollow accounts that post promotional content, are overly negative, or that are designed to distract rather than inform you.

BOX 6.1: FOLLOWING, FOLLOWERS, CONNECTION

Social media platforms use "following" to describe the act of subscribing to someone's updates, and "followers" for the people who have chosen to subscribe to yours. As a default practice on most platforms, you can follow anyone without them approving your follow. If you follow someone who also follows you, you are each "mutuals".

LinkedIn uses the same terminology as the other platforms, but also uses the term "connection" to refer to a mutual relationship where both parties have agreed to connect. A connection on LinkedIn is effectively the same as being "mutuals", but often signals a closer professional relationship.

Customising your social feeds

All social media platforms have a default newsfeed that is the first thing you see when you enter the social media's URL address in the browser on your computer, or when you open the app on your phone. The newsfeed is an updating stream of posts, videos, and updates—curated by the social media platforms' algorithms based on your interests, your interactions on the platform, and the people you follow and are connected to. Box 6.2 gives one example of how to curate this default newsfeed in a conscious way.

BOX 6.2: YOUR FEED IS A STAKEHOLDER MAP

To get the most out of social media you need to go beyond just scrolling passively on that newsfeed that the social media platform happens to serve you. You need to continuously reprogramme the feed to adjust what you see. By curating who and what to follow with intention, your feed becomes a personal, real-time dashboard of the conversations and people that matter to your work.

Maria Theresa Norn, a researcher in entrepreneurship and *Associate Professor at the Technical University of Denmark*, is deliberate about this process. "I've spent a lot of time curating the list of people I follow", she explains. "And I routinely also go in and look at that list again and think: Are there people, organizations missing? Are there perspectives missing?"

Maria Theresa's feed includes policy officials (both high-level and mid-level), industry actors, journalists, funders, NGOs, and fellow academics—all speaking in their own distinct ways. The principle is simple but powerful: who you follow determines who you're listening to.

Strategic listening like this requires patience and intentional effort. "People get frustrated when they start a new platform and feel like it's taking forever", Maria Theresa reflects. "For me it's taken three, four months each time—and that's with effort. But over time, your feed starts to speak back to you".

By treating your feed as a stakeholder map—carefully tuned to both relevance and range—something interesting happens, according to Maria Theresa. You begin to sense shifts in language, attention, and agendas across sectors in real time. "If there's too much noise in your feed, you lose focus again". But when the balance is right, your feed becomes a research tool in its own right.

Your social media feed isn't just something that happens to you—it's a strategic choice about how you are connected to the world beyond your immediate research environment.

But you can also go beyond the default newsfeed. To optimise your incoming information flow, you can set up multiple high-quality, tailored feeds that are relevant for the particular process that you are working on at the specific time when you need it.

As you will see in the following examples, using your desktop computer for this is, in terms of managing information flows, generally superior to using the social media's own mobile apps.

Lists, or curated feeds, of useful people

One of the most important ways to curate information flows is to deliberately restrict this flow to a specific set of people. A list is a curated feed that only shows posts from specific accounts that you have selected.

You may follow hundreds of people on a social media platform, as you may have many varied professional and non-professional interests. Your algorithmically generated standard newsfeed when you first open the app will therefore show posts about widely different things. But with lists, you can restrict your newsfeed so that you only see posts from specific people when you are in the specific work mode where these people are relevant to you.

You can, for example, have lists of researchers in your own specific field, participants at a conference you just attended, potential research project collaborators, journalists in your field, relevant policymakers, and academic institutions that you know regularly post jobs relevant to you.

Some social media platforms like Bluesky, Mastodon, and X have the lists functionality as a standard feature. You just click a button in the lists menu point, give the list a name, and manually start adding names.

Lists can be either private, so only you know who is on the list, or public, where the people you put on a list get a notification.

Platforms differ in what they allow. On X, you can opt to make your lists either private or public. On Bluesky, your lists are public. On Mastodon, your lists are private.

LinkedIn makes things a bit more difficult. Here you have to set up a workaround (see Box 6.3 on the LinkedIn "a" list).

BOX 6.3: THE LINKEDIN "A" LIST

LinkedIn does not have a lists function so that you can have separate news-feeds for specific groups of people. But there is a workaround.

- Write "a" in the search field
- Click "posts"
- Click "sort by" and choose "latest"
- Click "from member" then add the first person's name you want
- Click "All filters", scroll down and start to add names
- Click "show results"
- Bookmark this URL in your browser
- Name the list as something that you will remember
- Have a folder in your browser with all your lists for easy access

Saved searches: Hashtags

Another way to deliberately design the information flow on social media platforms is to use hashtags (see Box 3.1) and keywords. The "#" or hashtag lets users cross-reference content by topic or theme.

This allows you to bookmark a hashtag, or a combination of hashtags in the platform's search field—and this will then list all the posts that have this hashtag combination.

A conference, for example, might urge participants to use a specific hashtag when posting on social media. The hashtag allows other participants to see all the posts from this conference on this particular social media platform just by clicking on the hashtag. An early example was #AOM2013 as the hashtag for the annual conference of the Academy of Management in 2013, which actively promoted the use of the hashtag and provided a list of top tweeters during the conference.

Researchers spontaneously converge upon specific hashtags, and combinations of hashtags, for research fields and objects of study, as in "#geology #volcano".

All of this means that you can set up combinations of searches that include the hashtags relevant to you in the search field of the platform and bookmark this search in your browser for easy access.

Saved searches: Keywords and Google dorks

The trouble with hashtags is that you are dependent on other users deliberately tagging their posts with a specific hashtag for you to be able to see it. You may therefore miss posts that are relevant to you, but where the user has simply not used a hashtag that is in your search. There may also be confusion or misalignment of the exact hashtag to use, such as #WOIC2025 and #WOIC25, which both refer to the World Open Innovation Conference in 2025.

To get around this, you can simply find combinations of keywords that are relevant to you (see Box 6.4) and bookmark a search with this combination on your browser. This bookmarked URL will then be an access point to the platform, in effect creating an alternative newsfeed that is relevant to you.

BOX 6.4: KEYWORD SEARCHES

By writing keywords or phrases in a social media platform's search field, you can unearth all of the posts on the platform that have this combination of words and phrases.

You can exploit this to set up multiple, alternative newsfeeds that are focused on your research interests and that show you posts from people outside your network.

By experimenting with combinations of keywords, you can find combinations that deliver new, interesting newsfeeds that you can bookmark in your browser. These are then your new entrances to the platform, avoiding the algorithmically rendered home newsfeed.

A chemist, for example, might have a keyword search on LinkedIn of "polyurethane" AND "chemical recycling". This will render all the posts that have the word polyurethane and the two-word phrase "chemical recycling" in them. She can then have a routine where she follows and interacts with the people who post interesting posts there.

Platforms differ in terms of which operators you can use in your search, but most of the basic Boolean operators work on most platforms, like AND (to include multiple terms), OR (to search for one term or another), NOT (to exclude terms), quotation marks ("") (for exact phrases), and parentheses (to group terms).

You can then repeat this exercise for a different relevant combination of keywords. Ideally, you will have a folder in your browser with multiple URLs, each with different names, each with different combinations of keywords, and each highly relevant to you. These are your only access points to the platform and will enable you to avoid the standard newsfeed and its distractions.

Finding good combinations of keywords calls for creativity, lateral thinking, and your own domain expertise. Ask yourself: what are the words that will appear in social media posts that I want to see? You can combine a specific research field, a methodology, a technology that you are interested in, and an object of study. The best combinations of keywords should be wide enough to render some posts but narrow enough to avoid too many irrelevant ones.

Combining keywords in the platform's search field and bookmarking them as separate URLs works on most of the platforms that are professionally relevant for researchers. The platforms differ, but most standard Boolean queries work (for example, "geology conference" AND "tectonics" NOT "call for papers").

Another related technique to improve your information flow is to use the Google "dorking" technique, which is to use Google's own advanced search operators to dig up information on the social media platform that won't easily pop up on a search on the social media platform itself.

Using this technique and bookmarking the Google searches will give you a "newsfeed" that is actually a search engine results page. In our experience, these techniques can be good for one-off searches of people and posts, but are less relevant for a regular social media routine.

Social media management tools

The techniques described above—the use of lists, hashtags, keywords, and dorks—are all methods to better control your information flow. They effectively allow you to get around the social media platforms' algorithmically generated newsfeed and thereby let you take control over what you want to see, when you want to see it.

Paid social media management tools like Hootsuite and Buffer offer to partly do the same thing, and across multiple platforms, for the cost of a subscription. They help you curate your information flow by allowing you to filter content, ensuring that you see the most relevant posts without being overwhelmed by noise.

Social media management tools for specific platforms include DeckBlue for Bluesky, which is free, and X Pro (the former Tweetdeck), which works for X and which you have to pay for.

Social media management tools can combine other services in the same package, like streamlining the scheduling of posts, so that you can pre-write several posts to be released at different times and automate otherwise repetitive tasks (see Box 6.5).

BOX 6.5: SOCIAL MEDIA MANAGEMENT, DISCOVERY, AND AUTOMATION TOOLS

There are a range of social media management, content discovery, and automation tools available. Here are a few that academics commonly use:

- Buffer and Hootsuite let you schedule posts across multiple platforms and provide basic analytics.

- IFTTT (If This Then That) and Zapier create automated workflows between different apps and services.
- ContentStudio and SocialBee help with content discovery and curation.
- Feedly, Inoreader, and RSSHub aggregate content from journals and news sources relevant to your field.

Groups and closed communities

Some social media platforms have a group, or community, functionality, like LinkedIn Groups or Facebook Groups, that function as private or semi-private spaces where researchers with a shared interest can connect, discuss, and share resources.

Groups are often centred around academic research, industry trends, or job opportunities within a specific research area. Because Groups are a gated community, they allow professionals and researchers to interact in a focused environment, without interruption from outsiders, making it easier to form valuable connections.

Groups typically require that you are approved for membership by the administrator of the Group. This means that the posts and comments within the Group are more serious and focused than on general social media feeds. An example of a LinkedIn Group is "Veterinary Epidemiology and Biostatistics". It's listed as a public group, meaning anyone can view the posts, but only approved members can contribute. By contrast, private groups require membership both to view and to post.

Other social media platforms that offer Groups or Community functionality include Reddit, with "subreddits" on topic-based discussions with moderators, and Mastodon, where its Instances are somewhat similar to Groups in that communities emerge around specific interests.

Bluesky and X do not have anything that corresponds to a traditional closed group or community function.

Taming notifications

A notification is an alert or message from a platform that informs you about updates, interactions, or activities related to your account or network. They can pop up on your phone screen, typically as a red dot on the app's icon on your phone screen, or as an email notification in your inbox.

They are designed to distract you from the job at hand and entice you onto a platform when you are doing something else, and they will typically not help you to be productive in your work. Avoiding notifications may therefore be the smart thing to do, or at least you should find a way to manage them. This is in line with our suggestion (in the section "Time slots and deep work") to schedule dedicated time to be on social media.

Some social media platforms do a better job of providing useful notifications than others. For example, some of LinkedIn's notifications may be valuable to you, but this will not always be the case—which makes it difficult to say no to all of them. One example is when you get a direct message notification from LinkedIn. In most cases, you could easily wait to read this message until the scheduled time slot when you plan to work on LinkedIn (see more below). But many of us, including the authors, are just too curious to be able to turn it off—or we may be afraid to miss an important message.

Finding the optimal settings to stay informed while minimising distractions is difficult, and we suspect that more researchers on social media are "over-notified" rather than "under-notified" with notifications. This is because social media platforms typically enable all notifications by default, leaving it up to the user to turn them off after creating an account.

So, what do you do? Our recommendation, if you are being distracted by notifications, is to turn them *all* off for the platform. Then, if you find that you are missing updates that are valuable to you, selectively turn on each specific type of notification, such as, for example, direct messages, if you deem them important.

Time slots and deep work

By customising your social feeds via lists, saved searches or social media management tools, and by opting out of most notifications, you can regain your agency as a researcher.

Another way is to deliberately have daily or weekly time slots to be on the social media platforms and to consciously avoid going back to them at any other time.

This planning of your social media work time demands self-discipline, especially for those social media users who are already attuned in their daily routine to ongoing social media conversations. Box 6.6 offers a sample social media routine for a minimal one hour a week of social media use.

You may be more comfortable with a shorter daily slot if it, for example, fits into your daily commute. But the advantage of a longer, weekly slot is that it nudges you towards long-term planning and thinking, and away from distraction.

BOX 6.6: A SAMPLE SOCIAL MEDIA ROUTINE

The following is what a weekly, one-hour social media routine might look like.

Time slot: Friday 8–9 am, at the start of the working day. Tasks that last longer than one hour are done over consecutive Fridays. On other days, you only allow yourself short bursts of time to react to important comments and direct messages.

Within the Friday time slot, go through the following checklist:

- Monitor your research field through keyword and list searches on all platforms.
- Retweet, repost, share, tag relevant others to posts that you find, and offer help to others.
- Prepare (complicated) own posts (defer to next Friday if you are not finished).
- Set up of new accounts, schedules, and routines (defer if you can't do this within the hour).

Limiting your social media attention to specific time slots goes against the intentions of social media platforms. These platforms, in particular the microblogging social media like Bluesky, Mastodon, and X, are designed for real-time, unplanned updates. And a response to what is going on in your field in real time can generate visibility and a window of opportunity for conversations that your planned posts will never achieve.

But for many researchers, planning a specific time slot for social media work is the *only* way to maintain a social media presence without it becoming a distraction. The approach makes sense from a deep work perspective. It keeps your profile active, enables a degree of networking and ideation, and removes the pressure of thinking up content on the spot.

That said, there may be another routine that fits you well, depending on your goals and context. In any case, to get the most out of social media you need to balance two contradictory aspects: the time slots for longer social media tasks and the real-time moments that foster energetic, genuine, and spontaneous conversations (see also Chapter 10).

One way to get the best of both worlds is to work on a weekly plan as in Box 6.6, but then to allow yourself short bursts of time to check in and react—especially around conferences, big debates, or major research developments in your field.

On-platform scheduling of posts

One of the ways in which social media platforms keep you coming back is through the gratification from seeing other users giving you "likes", commenting, and otherwise reacting to your post. For researchers, this can be a distraction. Say you have looked forward to updating your network with a link to your new publication, it's only human to want to return to the platform within a few minutes to see if anyone in your network has reacted to your post.

Returning to see if anyone has reacted is good if it comes from a desire to interact with the people who comment and converse on your post. But it's unhealthy when it becomes a form of validation and distraction in itself.

One way to avoid this is to deliberately schedule your posts to be released at a specific time in the future. In this way, you cognitively separate the creative work time that you have put into the post from the time when it's released on the platform and seen by your network. Most of the time, you will have largely forgotten about the post by the time it comes out, effectively sidetracking the need to return to the platform to check up on it. If you have set up your notifications correctly, you should only be reminded of the post if someone comments on it, asking for your response.

Scheduling posts for release at a later time also allows you to batch your tasks by working on multiple posts at the same time, but with their release on the platform at different time slots, thereby avoiding the effect of crowding your network's feeds with your posts.

Ideally, posts should be scheduled for release at a time slot before your potential network is likely to be on the platform, as this makes it more likely that they will see the post when they are there. The time when it's most rational to post is especially relevant for the microblogging platforms, as posts here will generally have a shorter "half-life" or time when they are visible to the people that follow you before being crowded out by other posts on your network's newsfeeds. For other platforms like LinkedIn, the time when your post comes out is slightly less relevant. Here, the post's half-life will be longer, especially if you have tagged the people whom you think will find the post interesting.

LinkedIn and X allow you to schedule posts natively on their own platforms, while you can typically only schedule posts on other platforms by using third-party social media management tools (see Box 6.6).

7

PRODUCTIVITY

Automation and AI in academic social media

> NotebookLM is just one of the tools that can break open research that would otherwise stay locked in specialist language.
> —Jan Recker, Professor for Information
> Systems at the University of Hamburg

The automation paradox

As an academic, you suffer from an almost continuous lack of time. There are already too many tasks. After lab or field work, writing papers, applying for grants, teaching, mentoring, and committee work, you may feel it's impossible to also maintain an effective social media presence. If you are an early-career researcher, you may be under further pressure, having to juggle short-term contracts and uncertainty about the next step in your career. You may have the additional burden of balancing your family and childcare responsibilities. Yet, as we emphasise throughout this book, social media are nevertheless important channels for research dissemination, networking, ideation, and co-creation (see Chapter 2). In this sense, social media activity should be considered an integrated part of your broader set of tasks. Indeed, many individual tasks—like updating your network on your progress or inviting people to a seminar—are more efficient with social media than without.

Still, the tension in terms of time pressure has led many scholars to consider automation as part of their social media strategy and way of working. Automation tools have been developed especially for the dissemination function of social media, and they involve using the tools to write posts, schedule posts, and manage your online presence with less manual effort. The idea is that you can maintain a consistent, professional social media presence with a fraction of the time investment. With the advent of AI-powered tools based on large language models (LLMs), such as ChatGPT, Claude, Gemini, and Copilot, this kind of

DOI: 10.4324/9781003589341-7

support has become even more accessible and appealing. In Box 7.1, we offer an example of how AI tools can transform academic texts to other formats, including social media-ready formats, thereby making knowledge accessible to non-academic practitioners.

BOX 7.1: IMPACT SUPERPOWERS

LLM-based AI tools, or chatbots, are giving researchers a new capability on social media: the ability to reframe complex research for the people who actually need it.

For *Jan Recker, Professor for Information Systems at the University of Hamburg*, this is where the real potential lies: not in churning out lots of research-related posts on social media, but in transforming dense academic material into formats that are made to travel—on LinkedIn, in classrooms, in inboxes, or across industry networks.

"An academic paper behind a paywall might get a few hundred clicks. That's considered a success. But that's not reach—not in any real sense", he says. Achieving real impact requires translation into other formats and contexts that have more public exposure.

An example of this is Jan's use of tools like Google's *NotebookLM* to generate short, conversational podcast scripts directly from his academic papers. "It's perfect for teaching, press outreach, and posting on social media. NotebookLM is just one of the tools that can break open research that would otherwise stay locked in specialist language".

Jan uses the phrase "translational" for this process: LLMs "translate" or reframe academic writing to other formats, including social media-ready formats, thereby making research accessible in the places where practitioners and other audiences are already spending their time.

Jan also mentions some other positive uses of AI tools for social media-mediated research impact:

- Helping non-native English-speaking researchers post confidently.
- Automating repetitive formatting tasks.
- Creating accessible "hooks" to help let your deep, complex work surface on noisy social media feeds.

But there is a paradox at the heart of all automation of academic social media. The very qualities that make social media valuable for scholars—authentic connection, serendipitous discovery, meaningful dialogue—can be undermined by excessive automation. And although the developments in AI have given rise to more human-like automated messages (Mollick & Mollick, 2022), there remains a general concern about how to stay authentic in the social media age (Audrezet et al., 2020; Haimson et al., 2021). AI-powered tools may make posting easier, thereby also inadvertently leading to a massive increase in the sheer volume of posts, but they are not (yet) good at helping find that particular person who will get our research to matter (see Box 7.2).

BOX 7.2: USING AI TO FIND THE RIGHT PEOPLE

Social media platforms are good at connecting people—but not necessarily the people *you* need for your research to matter. Finding the right collaborator, policy official, or practitioner can be hard. Unless you already know exactly who you're looking for, you're often left sifting through noise.

To add to this problem, legacy platforms like LinkedIn and X have become gated communities, increasingly limiting—or monetising—access to third-party tools and data, making it even more difficult to find the right people. Data-savvy academics can experiment with spreadsheets and things like customised GPTs to filter bios and job roles: but platform restrictions still apply.

"It's a problem waiting to be solved", says AI and communications strategist *Jesper Andersen, Founder of Quantum Public Relations.* "And it's a frustration in every profession—not just research".

There are workarounds. For finding other researchers, tools like Perplexity can serve as a kind of lightweight literature scan, he says: "If you said, I want to find other researchers who have written papers on the topic I'm currently investigating, Perplexity with the academic research criteria switched on would be a starting point".

But for professional or practice-based stakeholders outside academia, the challenge is tougher. What Jesper calls *horizon scanning*—a form of networked sense-making borrowed from business intelligence—might eventually offer a way forward.

The idea is powerful: instead of broadcasting posts and hoping the right people notice, researchers could proactively *map* their stakeholder field. AI tools could then make networking more targeted.

"I imagine something like this will eventually be part of LinkedIn's premium offer—but not yet. And certainly not across platforms".

In this chapter, we will address this paradox head-on. We will explore the range of automation tools available to academics, how they can be used effectively and ethically, and where the boundaries should be drawn. We will then turn to the emerging role of generative AI in academic social media, examining both its promise and limitations.

A spoiler alert: we believe that all social media automation tools should enhance rather than replace the human element of scholarly communication—quite like Holgersson et al. (2024) argue that AI may enhance, enable, or replace traditional open innovation practices. The goal isn't to become a robotic presence in the academic social sphere, but rather to use automation thoughtfully, in service of more meaningful interactions with others.

Social media automation for academics

At its most basic level, automation of social media in an academic context means using tools to perform repetitive social media tasks without direct human intervention at the moment of execution.

In previous chapters, we have already mentioned examples of low-level, simple automation of social media processes like:

- Scheduling a post announcing a paper to go live during peak engagement hours (Chapter 6).
- Cross-posting research threads, blog summaries, or event notices across multiple platforms (Chapter 5).
- Using tools to discover relevant literature, funding calls, or policy news.
- Analytics tracking to measure engagement on publications (Chapter 2).

In recent years, the development of generative, LLM-based, chatbots like ChatGPT has dramatically improved the ability of many researchers to quickly:

- Draft social media posts in different formats (see Box 7.3), like summaries for non-experts, threads of posts from conferences, and explainers based on complex research content.
- Render simple illustrations and infographics related to science.
- Make graphics for invitations to conferences, seminars, etc.

BOX 7.3: AI TOOLS FOR VISUALS, SUMMARIES, AND CURATION

Generative AI can help translate your research into more interactive, multimedia formats beyond text. Here are the key categories of tools to explore:

- **Visualisation tools**: Turn data into shareable graphics or charts. Tools like Tableau, Flourish, or ChatGPT with Code Interpreter (Advanced Data Analysis) can help generate visuals from raw data or tables.
- **Summarisation tools**: Extract key points from your papers to make them accessible to wider audiences. Try Scholarcy or HumataAI for automatic summaries or ChatGPT to tailor summaries for different platforms (e.g., a LinkedIn post vs. a conference pitch).
- **Image and video generation tools**: Create illustrations, figures, or animations that bring abstract concepts to life. DALL-E, Runway, and Midjourney (via Discord) can generate images based on your prompts. For short explainer videos, tools like Pika or Lumen5 can help.
- **Curation and discovery tools**: Find relevant conversations or new papers in your field. ResearchRabbit and Connected Papers let you explore networks of research. Feedly (with Leo AI) helps track news and updates in specific domains.

These tools can expand your reach and save time, but use them critically. The best results are achieved when you use these tools as a starting point, and then layer on your own expertise and voice.

Automation of social media processes has several benefits for you as an individual researcher. Automation can increase your posting consistency and thereby "reach"—the number of people who see your post on a newsfeed. If everything else were equal, this is valuable, as with more people seeing your updates, the chance your work will have an influence where it matters is higher.

A more consistent social media presence through scheduling tools can lead to a growth in your audience, measured in follower numbers, compared to sporadic manual posting. However, excessive automation can also come at the cost of not being perceived as authentic, which is a key part of making social media work (Marwick & boyd, 2011).

Automation ranges from lightweight assistance (like scheduling a post to appear when your audience is most active) to full replacement of human judgement (allowing AI to generate content without review). Where your own social media automation practices fall on this spectrum should depend on your goals, audience, and ethical boundaries.

AI tools for multilingual academic communication

One of the most promising applications of chatbots built on LLMs in academic social media is the breaking down of language barriers. Academia has long faced criticism for its Anglo-American dominance, with English-language publications receiving disproportionate attention and citation rates (Liu, 2017). This has given an unfair advantage to English-language fluent academics.

While most research communication still happens in English, AI is making it easier to bridge the language disadvantage felt by non-native English speakers. Translation tools powered by AI are now capable of translating academic content into multiple languages in seconds. You can use these tools to:

- Translate your posts in real time, reaching broader audiences.
- Respond to comments or questions in languages you don't speak.
- Analyse your audience's language preferences to tailor your content.

Many platforms now offer a "translate" option on posts, making it easier for academics in non-English-speaking countries to post in their own language, knowing that everyone can read their post with one extra click. Tools like DeepL make it easier to formulate posts in multiple languages. The tool does not automate the process end-to-end, but translation is becoming a more fluid part of preparing posts. Similarly, AI tools can help academics engage with comments and questions in languages they don't speak fluently, enabling global conversations around research. These developments have the potential to widen the academic conversations on social media threads.

At the time of writing, these tools are not perfect. They can miss subtle meanings or mistranslate technical terms. To avoid misunderstandings, it's a good idea to have a colleague review translated content, especially if it's important or sensitive. But that said, AI translation is already making your research more accessible and inclusive—opening up new collaborations and readerships far beyond your usual networks.

The authenticity challenge of AI-augmented communication

Generative AI tools can draft posts, summarise research, brainstorm ideas, and simulate human conversation. But their use raises an important question: how do you stay authentic when a machine is doing some of the talking?

We believe that the key is to treat AI as a collaborator, not a ghost-writer. Let it help structure your ideas, but always use *your* voice and your critical thinking. Here are a few practical tips:

- Use an AI chatbot to draft, not to write: Let it help you get started, but finish the post yourself.
- Disclose your AI contributions: If a post was significantly shaped by AI, consider mentioning it. Being open can increase trust.
- Double-check everything: Chatbots can 'hallucinate'—especially when summarising research. Constantly fact-check.
- Draw a line: Some types of interaction—like responding to complex feedback—should always be done by you.

Ultimately, your audience wants to hear from *you* and your unique perspective—not polished "content". The chatbots should simply help you express yourself better.

AI tools for graphics, images, and curation

Apart from drafting text for posts and translation, generative AI tools can also help turn your research into other formats like images and graphics to communicate your research more effectively (see Box 7.3).

Some academics use curation tools to find papers and content that they can reshare from their own account, thereby turning themselves into hubs for content within their own field. The AI-enhanced curation tools can help surface ideas, but let your expertise decide what to share.

Ultimately, you should add your voice to everything you post. It's only relevant for your followers if you explain why it matters or how it connects to your work. And don't forget to watch how people respond and make adjustments accordingly. Thoughtful curation combined with personal commentary is one of the most effective ways to build a credible presence on academic social media.

Automation should fit a sustainable routine

The purpose of automation and assistance from generative AI tools should be a sustainable routine—a social media practice that can be maintained alongside your lab, fieldwork, writing, and teaching responsibilities without it leading to burnout or forcing you to make compromises on quality.

If using social media starts to feel like another full-time job, it's time to rethink your approach. In Chapter 6, we outlined our recommendations for delimiting social media work into daily or weekly time slots to safeguard your (other) research work.

Automation and generative AI tools in your social media work can be a key part of keeping this delimited schedule. For this end, you can:

- Identify automation candidates in your social media routines: look for repetitive tasks that don't require your unique expertise or voice.
- Start scheduling: Scheduling tools reduce the daily burden of social media maintenance by allowing you to batch your work and automate the publication of your posts.
- Add automation tools gradually: measure the impact of these tools on your time, your engagement metrics, and the authenticity of your interactions.

Ethical automation

Automation can offer practical solutions to many tasks for academics on social media. But how do you use it without compromising your authenticity or values?

With automatically generated texts everywhere, audiences tend to scroll past what they perceive as polished chatbot posts and formats that they don't recognise as coming from a real person. What draws them in is when they know someone is actually there. People want to hear from you, not a faceless content machine. So, any use of automation should support, not replace, your voice. See Box 7.4 for some principles for building an ethical and effective automation routine.

BOX 7.4: PRINCIPLES FOR ETHICAL AND EFFECTIVE AUTOMATION

Using automation can streamline your social media efforts, but only if applied thoughtfully. These principles can help you stay both efficient and authentic:

- **Be transparent**: It's fine to use scheduling tools like Buffer or Later, but don't pretend everything is happening live. Occasionally noting that a post was pre-scheduled builds trust and credibility.
- **Maintain oversight**: If you use templates or AI tools (like ChatGPT) to draft posts, always review and personalise before publishing. Your content should sound like you, not like a bot.
- **Set boundaries**: Some things shouldn't be automated. Always respond personally to complex questions, criticism, or sensitive feedback.
- **Make space for real conversations**: Automated posts aren't a substitute for interaction. Set aside time to respond to comments and engage meaningfully with your community.
- **Review your tools**: Digital platforms and APIs (the set of rules that let different platforms talk to each other) change frequently. Reassess your automation setup regularly to ensure it still supports your goals.

Thoughtful automation isn't about doing less—it's about focusing your time where it matters most: authentic connection.

There are many automation tools available (see also Box 6.5), from basic scheduling on social media management platforms to systems that integrate with your email, RSS feeds, or even data sources. Start simple, build confidence, and scale only when it makes sense.

Finally, it's worth considering the broader ethical implications of automation in academic communication. As scholars, you are not just content creators but also stewards of public knowledge. This means that *how* we communicate matters as much as *what* we communicate. Over-reliance on automation can blur the lines between genuine conversations and a performative presence, potentially eroding trust not only in your voice but in academic voices in general. It contributes to the homogenisation of post content, language, and styles, where nuanced or critical perspectives get drowned out by algorithm-friendly formats. Being mindful of these dynamics is part of our ethical responsibility as academics. A thoughtful automation strategy should not only serve to make you more efficient as an individual, but also uphold the values of openness, integrity, and intellectual contribution that define scholarly work.

The human–machine balance in academic social media

Automation and generative AI offer powerful tools for academics seeking to maintain an impactful social media presence while managing limited time. From scheduling posts to translating content for global audiences to using AI as a thought partner, these technologies can significantly enhance productivity.

At the same time, we have emphasised the continued importance of authentic human connection. The most successful academic social media users strike a thoughtful balance: using automation to handle routine tasks while preserving their unique voice as a scholar.

This balance will look different for each of you. It depends on your field, career stage, audience, and personal preferences. The frameworks and strategies we've outlined are meant to be adapted to your specific circumstances.

As these technologies continue to evolve, it's worth remembering that the fundamental purpose of academic social media remains to connect researchers with each other and with wider audiences, to share knowledge, and to advance scholarly discourse. Technology should serve these goals, not replace or distort them.

8

CHALLENGES

Navigating the dark side of social media

> I hadn't been on my phone, and then suddenly, pings and pings and pings.
>
> —Julia Andreasen, PhD researcher in
> glaciology at the University of Minnesota

When things take off—and go sideways

In previous chapters, we have mostly described academics' social media use in positive terms as a no-risk activity. In this chapter, however, we address some of the challenges. We look first at some of the risks that come from public exposure. For a minority of unfortunate researchers, even innocuous communication actions can provoke disproportionate backlash, viral storms, misinterpretation, or even harassment on social media—Box 8.1 and Box 8.7 offer examples of this.

Many more researchers experience small-scale controversies and conflict. And they often touch on the academic identities, roles, and expectations that people have of you as a scientist. So, in this chapter, we offer a framework for responding to critical comments and look at how confusion can arise from academic identities and roles as experts, communicators, policy pundits, and public intellectuals.

BOX 8.1: ICE *SHELF* OR ICE *SHEET*:
IT IS ALL IN A WORD

They had little prior expectation that their research would "go anywhere", recalls glaciologist *Julia Andreasen, PhD researcher at the University of Minnesota*. After all, she and her co-authors were "just filling in a data gap". But then suddenly, "in the car on the way home from a memorial

---

DOI: 10.4324/9781003589341-8

service, I started getting notifications. I hadn't been on my phone, and then suddenly, pings and pings and pings", she remembers.

Her co-authored 2023 paper examining changes in Antarctic ice shelf area was suddenly at the centre of a wave of misinformation on social media by climate sceptics (Andreasen, 2025).

Their study found that ice shelves grew in the period 2009–2019—an observation with no direct link to climate change. An ice *shelf* floats on the ocean and regularly gains and loses size in a balance of snow accumulation, ice flow, and iceberg calving. The ice sheet, on the other hand, is grounded ice that can melt in response to climate change and contributes to sea-level rise.

But that nuance was lost online. A sentence in their abstract was pulled out of context and used to question the reality of climate change. "What's actually melting: The climate hoax narrative", wrote one tweeter on X and set off a train of retweets and reposts that had Julia and her colleagues' work going viral for all the wrong reasons.

At first, Julia felt the need to respond, explaining the science and correcting the misinterpretations. But as the controversy escalated, she realised that many of those engaging in the online discussion were not genuinely interested. "At first, I was replying to comments and emails, thinking, 'Okay, these are genuine questions.' But I never heard anything back. It felt fruitless".

Seeing an opportunity to learn from the controversy and contribute to broader conversations about science communication, Julia wrote up her experiences in the science news magazine Eos (Andreasen, 2025).

Looking back, Julia says that finding herself in a misinformation storm was not all bad: the controversy has ultimately made their study widely read, including among other scientists. "Our original article is now way up there on the list of highly downloaded climate-related articles. My advisor joked that if you wanted attention, this was the way to do it".

Julia Andreasen's advice:

- *Anticipate potential misunderstandings* or deliberate misinterpretations in article abstracts.
- Only *selectively debate with deliberate misinformers*—not all misinformation is worth addressing (see also the section "A framework for responding to critical comments" in this chapter). Work with fact-checkers and journalists to reframe discussions instead.
- *Track public reception* of your work, and publish follow-ups to clarify findings.

Researchers do not all face the same level of risk. For example, we are acutely aware that our own experience as (male) authors is from within a privileged Western academic community, where a misstep on social media will generally—albeit not always—have little personal consequence. This may not be the case for, say, women researchers in Eastern Africa (see Box 8.2). While some may only ever experience a mild online dispute, others may experience harassment, censorship, or even threats to their personal safety. These risks are disproportionately distributed to researchers from controversial fields, women, and regions with low levels of academic autonomy (Gosse et al., 2021; Veletsianos et al., 2018).

BOX 8.2: STANDING UP TO THE EVIL EYE

According to a Somali proverb, the human eye "can break through stone and steel". It refers to the "evil eye", a widespread belief in parts of the Middle East and Africa that being visibly successful can attract a curse inspired by other people's envy.

According to Somali-Dutch anthropologist *Sahra Ahmed Koshin, Executive Director of Somali Gender Hub*, overt self-promotion on social media in this part of Africa is seen as an invitation to bad fortune and—especially for women—digital harassment.

Sahra's own blogging and social posts from Somalia—accounts of development work and women's roles—have earned her a large, engaged audience, also among the Somali diaspora, with tens of thousands of followers on LinkedIn and X.

"Many women I know have revealed some sort of experience with sexist cyber hate speech. It doesn't matter whether you are veiled or not, once you 'cross the boundary', you will be trolled", she writes in a piece in The Guardian (Koshin, 2024).

Sahra says that her own social media routine has evolved into a cautious, more thoughtful curation. But she believes women need to speak out, and that the use of social media has in itself paved the way for a new culture of solidarity, community, and self-reliance among Somali women, wherever they live.

She offers the following advice to female researchers in exposed locations:

- Be part of a wider platform of other researchers—it makes you less of a target.
- Never announce your location beforehand.
- Stream live events, after the event, with a delay, so that your physical location is somewhere else.

Female researchers on social media in these regions should:

- Maintain norms of respect and decency when dealing with other women online.
- Raise awareness of cyberbullying and address the mental and psychological harm it causes.

In this chapter, we will present a set of personal, professional, and ethical strategies that can help you navigate social media's challenges without losing your voice.

Exposure and vulnerability

At their best, social media platforms are boundary-spanning technologies (see Chapter 2) that allow you to connect with other researchers, practitioners, policymakers, and citizens. For most of us, most of the time, these are positive interactions. At their worst, however, social media platforms can expose some of us to misunderstandings, hostility, risks to our reputation, and—if you live in a region with low academic autonomy—even threats to your freedom and livelihood (see, for example, Box 8.2).

By discussing and sharing your own and others' ongoing work and research, you become visible to other researchers, but also potentially to anyone else who has an interest in it. Social media expose you to others beyond your field, and to unknown audiences with other domains of expertise and interpretations.

Part of this is due to context collapse (see Box 8.3), and this can be a particular problem in some social science and humanities fields where the technical terminology, academic concepts, or objects of investigation are referred to in phrases that can be misunderstood or highly politicised.

BOX 8.3: KEY TERM: CONTEXT COLLAPSE

Context collapse is when a social media post that was originally intended for a specific audience is exposed to other, unintended audiences.

For researchers, this is typically when research-focused posts are interpreted outside of their own disciplinary context. The misinterpretations can be by trolls or campaigners for particular political agendas, which can lead to misunderstandings and backlash.

Context collapse occurs more often in:

- Highly politicised fields.
- Fields where research methods are controversial.
- Fields where the objects of study are contested.

Take the following (purely fictional) example: You are a social scientist researching diversity and inclusion practices in European corporations. You have just published a peer-reviewed article in a reputable journal, and you are genuinely proud of your work. It's data-driven, nuanced, and contributes to ongoing debates around corporate responsibility. You post the following on LinkedIn with a link so that readers can read more:

"In our study of diversity and inclusion practices across 9 EU countries, we found that well-intended inclusion efforts often backfire when 'one-size-fits-all' policies are exported across borders. Local context matters".

Your post is read by a few of your peers in your academic circles, and you receive some thoughtful questions. But then, two days later, a large account on Facebook with a big following outside academia shares a screenshot of your post with the comment: "Woke academics now say inclusion is *bad* if it's too inclusive. Can't make this up".

Suddenly, people start tagging you on other platforms. Strangers misread your nuance as ideology and conceive it as academic elitism. You are put on a list of "woke" scientists. A good colleague even suggests taking the original post down. But the post isn't wrong—it has just been misread.

This illustrates "context collapse". A post shared for one specific audience, in this case, fellow researchers interested in business practices, is suddenly exposed to unintended audiences.

What would you do yourself in the fictional example from above? Would you clarify in a further post? Delete the original post? Or do you just ignore it and let it all blow over? The social media platforms themselves offer a range of practices on the platform if you do decide to stop conversing (see Box 8.4), but how do you reach this decision in the first place?

BOX 8.4: BLOCK, MUTE ... OR JUST IGNORE

You don't have to argue your way out of conflict. Social media platforms allow you to limit conversations with people who harass you. They differ from platform to platform, but the concepts are the same.

Sometimes it is better to just *ignore*. It takes restraint, but not every post needs a response.

The *mute* or hide function on social media hides a user's posts and replies from *your* view without notifying them. It allows you to avoid seeing their posts without escalating the interaction.

The *block* function on social media prevents another user from viewing your posts or interacting with you, creating a boundary that ends further contact. As a researcher, however, the block function can put a researcher in a bad light, as the block can be screen-captured by your opponent, proving that you are unwilling to debate.

Harassment may be in breach of a social media platform's policies. In this case, a *report* allows you to flag posts or accounts to the platform's moderators for review.

In our experience, there is not one single correct answer in any of these situations. There is no set social media routine that will extricate you from all potential disputes and misunderstandings once they occur. Letting your work be visible as a researcher necessarily opens it up to other interpretations in different research and non-research contexts. And these new interpretations necessarily lead to you losing part of the control of the narrative around your work.

What you do have more control over on social media, however, are your own principles of truthfulness, approachability, and credibility. In the next section of this chapter, we set up a framework to help you uphold these principles in the context of a critical comment on your post.

A framework for responding to critical comments

In the following, we set out a *Reflective Response Framework* (summarised in Box 8.5) that you can use in connection with a critical comment or post referencing your work. It is a structured way for you to reflect and decide whether, how, and where to respond on social media. The framework is inspired by several sources, including Håhr Jensen (2022) and Lorentzen et al. (2019).

BOX 8.5: REFLECTIVE RESPONSE FRAMEWORK

How to decide whether—and how—to respond on social media.

Step 1: Who's talking?

- **Troll** ("happy") bad faith → Don't respond
- **Legitimate critic** ("provoked") good faith → Continue to step 2

Step 2: Choose where to respond

- **Conversation?** → Reply
- **Spiralling** or noisy thread in different networks or platforms? → Move to direct message/Reframe in new post
- **Hostile?** → Stay strategically silent

Step 3: Push or pull?

- **Push back** → Respectfully correct misrepresentation or false claims
- **Pull** → Re-express the critic's concern, clarify common ground, be curious and reflective

Step 4: Observe yourself

- **Check:** Would I be okay seeing my reply in a future context?

Step 1: Who's talking: Assess the intent

The first step is to evaluate the critic. Not all of them are deserving of your energy. For this, it is helpful to distinguish between trolls and legitimate critics. You can sense that *trolls* are "happy" provoking you and now want attention from you and others. Their critical comment is mostly for their own and their audience's gratification. A particularly insidious type of trolling is prevalent in academia, which goes under the name of "sealioning" (see Box 8.6), where someone repeatedly and insistently asks for further evidence, under the guise of academic civility—but in bad faith.

Unlike trolls, *legitimate critics* are in good faith. They are provoked by what they genuinely perceive to be a mistake or misreading on your part.

Trolls are performing their criticism for an audience, sometimes reframing your post into something that it didn't say. Legitimate critics, on the other hand, while they may be wrong in their interpretation, are genuinely interested in the subject at hand.

You should respond only to the legitimate critics, and not the trolls. A piece of folk wisdom from 1990s internet culture still holds true: trolls feed on visibility. Don't feed them.

Step 2: Choose where to respond: Decide where (or whether) to reply

The second step is to take a step back and think about where, and if, you will respond or respond further if the conversation has already started. Is this still a conversation—or has it become a performance? Has your post moved beyond your own network? Has it been quote-posted into a hostile or unfamiliar crowd?

If the conversation thread has shifted to a different network or platform, you can opt to reply via a direct message. This is if the critic seems legitimate, but the conversational space has become noisy. You can also respond with a new post if you want to reframe the conversation in your own words.

Finally, you can choose a strategic silence—not every comment deserves a reply.

Step 3: Push or pull: Decide how to respond

In step 1, we identified that the critic is a legitimate critic. In step 2, provided we did not opt for a direct message or strategic silence, we opted to reply with a comment or new post.

Now you should choose the tone and structure of your response. It should be either "push back" or "pull":

Push back is when the person unintentionally misrepresents your research or introduces false claims. Here is where you should push back clearly, respectfully, and without arrogance, as in: "That's not quite what the data shows. In fact, we found...".

Pull is when you recognise common ground with the critic and want to listen to their input. It is about drawing them into a productive conversation where you show that you yourself are open to re-assessing your own viewpoints. Restate their critique in your own words, acknowledge the concern, and offer clarification: "If I understand you correctly, you're raising the problem with x. That's a fair concern—here's how I approached it".

Step 4: Observe yourself: Look at your reply as a stranger would

Before replying or posting, imagine not just how your interlocutor, the critic, will read it, but how an unfamiliar, future observer might read it. Observers may see your post or reply without in-depth knowledge of your work, at a later time, and in another context. Your reply should not only be read generously by strangers as well as your followers, but also by an imaginary reader from the future.

Then your reply is ready to go.

To summarise: You need to protect your focus and maintain the kind of scholarly conversations that you yourself want to be a part of. The Reflective Response Framework outlined above is a tool to help you make this happen.

Role confusion: Scientist, expert, and citizen

As an academic, you are both a scientist, an expert, and a citizen. You are a *scientist* who advances the scientific enterprise through your own work and that relates to a field. You are an *expert* who has a deep knowledge of some object, phenomenon, circumstance, or concept. Each of these objects, phenomena, circumstances, or concepts relates to specific policies or issues that are debated in the public sphere, also on social media. And so finally, you are a *citizen* who participates in, relates to, and evaluates the wider society through the optics of your own viewpoint and expertise, but who is also swayed by your own biases and ideologies.

As human beings, we can have all these identities—scientist, expert, and citizen—merged into one. But in the social media space, it is expected that we take on the perspective of only one of these at a time.

In our experience, conflicts with both scientists and non-scientists come about when these roles are either confused by you, or your audience, or are not declared.

One of your social media posts that describes ongoing research on a phenomenon might inadvertently portray a hypothesis as a fact in which you have sole expertise. This might come off as arrogant to others who approach the same phenomenon from the perspective of another field. A social media post that flags your expertise fails to mention that you are speaking as an informed *citizen* among other informed citizens with conflicting viewpoints in a complex society.

BOX 8.6: KEY TERM: SEALIONING

Sealioning is a type of hostile, passive-aggressive trolling, where someone repeatedly and insistently asks for evidence, explanations, or further references under the guise of civility, but often in bad faith.

The goal is to wear the other person down, derail the conversation, or force them into an endless debate.

For researchers working in controversial fields, sealioning can be an exhausting form of harassment that appears civil on the surface but is meant to undermine or provoke.

Role confusion can often be *more* prevalent among senior scientists than early career researchers. Due to the prevalence of impostor syndrome among younger researchers, they tend to underestimate their own uniqueness and expertise within their field, leading to less research-related social media activity. This is a problem in its own right, leading them to miss out on the impact opportunities described in this book. But at least they don't underestimate the biases that come from many years of socialisation into their own field—biases that often lead them to devalue other perspectives and areas of non-academic professional expertise.

To counteract the confusion of roles, we recommend that you clarify the specific role you are taking on in your social media posts. Are you speaking as a *researcher*, involved in research that is in process? Are you speaking as an *expert* on something in the world, from your own research experience? Or are you speaking from your role as a *public intellectual*, speaking as a well-informed citizen?

Coping with conflict and controversy

Despite the best intentions, you may end up entangled in controversies on social media. Just like in other parts of your professional life, conflicts emerge unexpectedly, and at the worst possible times. The ecologist Pablo Manzano, for example, suddenly found himself the object of ridicule based on a 20-second video clip from a wide-ranging academic debate on rewilding (see Box 8.7).

BOX 8.7: WHEN THE WOLVES COME FOR YOU

It was a serious academic panel debate on the subject of rewilding in Madrid, Spain. But on social media, the argument spiralled out of control.

Ecologist *Pablo Manzano, Fellow* at the *Basque Centre for Climate Change BC3*, had briefly speculated on what would happen if predators like wolves were no longer shaped by human pressures. A 20-second video of this, clipped from a 2-hour-long debate, was shared by an activist-linked account on X that ridiculed him. Pablo, the post said, is afraid that wolves will eat his children and accused him of fearmongering, pseudoscience, and being beholden to the meat industry. Other accounts, some of them run by serious academics, piled on.

It then spilled onto another platform. One Instagram message read: "You're such a moron, anyone would attack you before a wolf even gets the chance." When Pablo protested, other academics then mocked him for playing the victim.

Rewilding and climate change are both "hot potato" issues on their own. When you combine the two, it is truly explosive. In another X comment thread on greenhouse gas emissions by wild herbivores and livestock, Pablo had to face up to activists who, in bad faith, repeated calls for new evidence, using sealioning debating techniques (see Box 8.6). Others then implied that when Pablo *did* reply, the fact that he continued to argue his point only proved that he was a "white privileged entitled arrogant man".

The spats reveal something deeper about how social media operate.

Pablo Manzano, still an avid professional social media user years on, reflects: "Social networks are on the one hand a source of potential for scientific exchange, like being in a permanent conference. But they are also a potential source of confrontation with users outside the scientific exchange context who have strong political positions and are activists. Climate debates are especially sensitive to this".

In the following, we offer a set of strategies to help you keep your personal and ethical bearings as a researcher on social media.

In the moment, disputes can be overwhelming. Especially if you are less experienced in research, they can lead you to question your own competence. And as they take place in public, it is as if any misstep is magnified.

But these disputes can also be seen positively. They can be testing grounds for your ideas, opportunities to refine your arguments, and—if your humility allows it—occasions to deepen your own understanding. The publicity of a hot contest on social media can, in itself, help cultivate intellectual curiosity among non-scientists and more generosity in the scientific community.

The following recommendations will not keep you immune from harm, but they will help you stay resilient, ethical, and open.

Always argue in good faith

Uphold your generosity, curiosity, and good faith even in hostile spaces, and even if your interlocutors do not. We will have more to say about generosity and kindness on social media in Chapter 9. But suffice to say here: Do not be arrogant towards critics. Your responses are not for the critics' consumption, but for other readers. Trust in your readers' intelligence—and be kind!

Resist the urge to "win"

It is easy to get drawn into arguments. This happens especially when a dispute has started politely but then evolved, or if your counterpart has got their facts wrong. At some point, the urge to win takes over. But especially when debating with commenters who are engaging in bad faith, trying to win an argument is playing into their hands. Winning is then actually losing. Unlike face-to-face conversations, outside observers will not necessarily wait until "the end" of a thread. What an outside observer sees is two people arguing. For this reason, make sure that each and every one of your comments and responses shows you in a good light.

Don't try to control the narrative

Scientific conversations on social media are open-ended and have unpredictable positive impacts that we are unaware of at the time the conversations take place. But they are also vulnerable to being re-scripted, especially by activists in fields that are surrounded by emotional or political controversy, and these are the ones that we become aware of, and that frustrate us. As in our Reflective Response Framework (see Box 8.5), you should limit your responses to those who discuss in good faith. Sometimes, evidence-based conversations are intercepted and pulled into new directions. They become chaotic, emotionally charged, and ideologically motivated. The logic shifts from scientific reasoning to moral accusations, identity politics, or emotional spectacle. As a researcher, what you can add to those intercepted discussions will be limited, so avoid them even if you disagree. Just let go!

If it is warranted, apologise

Sometimes you realise that you are partly to blame if a conversation has gone off track. It may have been unintentional—a poorly worded post, a misjudged joke, or a comment made without full context. If that's the case, a proportionate apology will de-escalate the tension with those who have argued with you in good faith. It also serves as a model for ethical practice that will serve as inspiration for others. The apology will also increase, not decrease, your standing with those not directly involved in the discussion.

Seek support from your colleagues

Many universities don't have designated staff to support researchers during social media conflicts. Advice typically comes from communications teams, which have their own institution's reputation as their priority. In practice, researchers often rely on informal peer support or their own judgement to navigate these moments. For this reason, it always helps to enlist the help of close colleagues. Just formulating the conflict with a trusted peer can clarify what's really going on and what kind of response, if any, is needed.

As we described in Chapter 2, social media are *boundary-spanning* technologies that link you to professionals in businesses and institutions, as well as to informed citizens. The conversations on social media are open-ended with unpredictable positive impacts. But this means that conversations can be re-scripted, sometimes deliberately. Still, we believe that the positive outcomes far outweigh these risks for most scientists. And in the next chapter, we will describe how social media can be used by researchers as a conscious force for good, to uphold a positive community.

9

GENEROSITY

Exploring the bright side of social media

> Invite others into conversations and recommend a junior colleague for a speaking slot.
>
> —Thomas Bandholm, Professor at the University of Copenhagen

Build the community you want to be a part of

If you just read our previous chapter on navigating controversy, you are probably in need of some motivation. After all, you might think, if sharing and discussing your own research and helping others with their research entails so many risks, then why bother at all?

But just as negativity is a part of the academic social media space—as it is in all spaces where humans converse—so is positivity in the form of kindness and generosity. Recent research in the field of archaeology has shown that positive sentiment and non-threatening language are more likely to be shared on social media, and that this counteracts the often-claimed negativity bias on these platforms, which emerges from audiences' selective attention to conflict and negativity (Bonacchi et al., 2025). We believe that kind and generous academic discourse should be replicated on social media and that it can be consciously learned and practised.

Kind and generous behaviour can be inspired by others' practical examples. So, after we explain in this chapter *why* academics have ethical obligations on social media, we will show you how you can switch to a kind mindset. We believe that academics should consciously move from a strategic, *what's-in-it-for-me* approach to a kind *what's-in-it-for-others* approach on social media.

We then offer you several practical ideas that can help you become a kinder and more generous practitioner on academic social media.

DOI: 10.4324/9781003589341-9

In the 2000 film *Pay It Forward* (IMDB, 2025), a social studies teacher assigns the class a plan that will change the world for the better. In his "pay it forward" plan, the recipient of a favour does a favour for three others rather than paying it back. Just like in the "pay it forward" scheme, we believe that your own kind and generous actions will not be in vain. Research validates this intuition. Neuroscience research demonstrates that prosocial behaviours—actions intended to benefit or help others—create measurable trust-building effects (Zak, 2017), while meta-analyses of organisational citizenship behaviours like helping colleagues show gains in productivity and efficiency, as well as reduced staff turnover (Podsakoff et al., 2009). Your generous actions will reinforce a ripple effect through what business researchers call "network effects" (Afuah, 2013)—where prosocial behaviours spread naturally and become self-reinforcing organisational assets (Grant, 2013). This creates inspiration for others and results in a more positive culture on academic social media, mirroring the documented benefits seen in high-performing organisations that systematically cultivate pay-it-forward attitudes.

Why academics should be kind on social media

As a scientist, you use social media because they are useful to *you*. As we have defined it in Chapter 2 and the "Reflective Model of Scientists' Social Media Use" (Table 2.1), the platforms help *you* communicate your work, let *you* meet interesting people to work with, inspire *you* with new ideas, and let *you* co-create with others.

But it is not all about *you*. The use of social media in academia entails obligations to others.

In recent years, there has been criticism of how social media can undermine our focus and mental health. This has led to what some have called a "digital backlash" (Albris et al., 2024). Academics, taking their cue from this, could opt to withdraw from social media to better concentrate on what they perceive as their "core research" work.

But if we only take a critical approach to social media use (see also Chapter 8), we are missing out on some of the most important facets of what social media can do, namely, help others. This is hardly ever addressed in the critical literature on social media, and especially not in literature like *Deep Work* (Newport, 2016)—as discussed in Chapter 6—that offers a way to increase academic personal productivity and satisfaction. By contrast, you could argue that there are ethical obligations to communicate your research in general and—by extension, on social media—even if it does reduce your productivity (which we don't believe has to happen).

In Table 2.1, our Reflective Model of Scientists' Social Media Use, we have, up until now, focused on the first row, the reasons and motivations for scientists' social media use. Now we can look beyond, at the mindful practices and ethical obligations that adhere to each of these reasons and motivations.

Let us start with the fundamental obligation to communicate your research. Most scientists would agree that it is a good thing when their scientific peers get to know about their work and results, as this is an integral part of the scientific process and is fundamental to how science progresses. Academic citations are a proxy for the entire modern scientific process, where scientists build on the work of others. If other scientists are to build on your work, they must have been made aware of it, and the continuous adding to the web of citations in scientific papers is the way that this happens.

Most scientists will—some of them grudgingly—agree that stakeholders, in the form of decision makers in the foundations and agencies that have funded their research, need to know what their money has been spent on.

Most scientists will moreover agree, in principle if not in practice, that the wider public needs to be able to get a general idea about the purpose and implications of their research if they so desire. Some scientists will even go beyond that and say that they are obliged to incite the curiosity of the general public to attract attention to their own field and to science in general. Communication with the general public not only makes it easier for scientists to do good science, but also ensures that the inclusion of youth in secondary schools will lead to promising new scientists joining their field in the future.

Many scientists do only the absolute minimum to satisfy the first two of these obligations on social media platforms. Communicating to peers and funders is arguably easier than communicating to a wider, more abstract set of stakeholders, such as non-academic domain experts or the general public—partly because you do not have a clear image of those with whom you are communicating.

One way of thinking about it is to consider your work a result of myriad decisions and favours from others. The fact that you are working on a subject that fascinates you, and that society wants you to do, should be something for which you are grateful. To top this, there are millions of people who have made your present scientific life possible: the designer of the power source for the high-energy beam in your experiment, the salesperson who originally negotiated with your university for a Microsoft package, the builder who cemented the bricks that keep you out of the rain, even the bus driver who transported you home from school many years ago. You have an obligation to show your gratitude to all these anonymous people. Involving and inciting the curiosity of other people on social media is one small way in which you can repay all those favours.

Many of us will dislike the posts about how (extremely) grateful someone is for a particular achievement when it comes across as a kind of "humblebragging"—bragging disguised as modesty. Posts (and certain people) on LinkedIn are particularly notorious for this—it has even fostered a whole concept called "LinkedIn cringe".

But there *is* an ethical obligation to communicate our work as a way of showing our gratitude. We are returning the *favour* that has been granted to us by all these unseen millions.

Within social media, there is also an ethical obligation to be kind and generous as a scientist, and this is where it gets interesting. Because the platforms that scientists use professionally are not necessarily designed for kindness and generosity, and the prevailing scientific culture on the platforms may not reinforce a kind and generous culture.

The legacy platforms that academics use, and that we analyse in this book, are fundamentally designed for individuals, not collectives. They are, for historically contingent and commercial reasons, oriented towards individual profiles and posts, and offer few affordances for co-creation. Box 9.1 below offers one way to counteract this.

BOX 9.1: LISTEN LIKE YOU'RE WRONG

What if social media use is an act of scientific humility, not just self-promotion?

Rehabilitation medicine scientist *Thomas Bandholm, Professor at the University of Copenhagen*, is acutely aware of how the academic system—and social media—rewards self-serving behaviours. While science is a collective endeavour, grants and promotions are awarded to individuals. Social media platforms then reinforce this individualism by rewarding self-promotional posts that focus on personal achievement.

Thomas is also one of the co-founders of the Excellence and Kindness in Research Training (ELIS) initiative—a collaborative training network that helps younger scientists do research with integrity and empathy. Some of its kindness principles can be applied to social media practices:

- Pursue excellence, but not at the expense of kindness.
- Focus on collective success more than personal success.
- Seek collaboration over competition.
- View vulnerability as courage—not imperfection.

In general, Thomas sees social media use as an opportunity to realign with deeper scientific values: generosity and curiosity.

"You can use the platforms differently", he says. Instead of just celebrating your own successes, you can add value by "sharing your slides, for instance. Or invite others into conversations. And recommend a junior colleague for a speaking slot".

For Thomas, it's about resisting platform culture in subtle, strategic ways. For example, you may decide to only follow those researchers who debate respectfully and who are willing to rethink their views. "The people I really value are the ones who can change their minds in public", he says, adding that scientists on social media should adhere to a principle popularised by Adam Grant: "Argue like you're right, listen like you're wrong".

Thomas' tips for kind social media use:

- Post to add value, not just visibility.
- Share slides or takeaways after talks.
- Recommend others for opportunities.
- Follow researchers who combine opinions with openness.
- Use your posts to model curiosity, not certainty.

Emergent cultures on the platforms reinforce this individualism and bragging about personal success. Let us use LinkedIn as an example. Scrolling down a newsfeed of scientists and academics, you get the impression that they only post about the grants and prizes that they have won. You would hardly ever see any posts coming from scientists posting about their disappointments, struggles, and insecurities. It can be depressing when you are surrounded by your more successful peers!

This is not entirely LinkedIn's fault: people do tend to post more about their successes than their failures. But then this bias for success is reinforced algorithmically by the platform. It works like this:

Say you give a "like" to a researcher colleague who has posted about winning a grant. You genuinely want to congratulate her. As a bare minimum, the LinkedIn newsfeed will in the future show you more content from this person, and more content with this type of post. Say you then, awkwardly, scroll past a post from a researcher colleague who has voiced their disappointment: maybe you didn't have the right emoji, maybe you felt something needed to be written in the comments, but you didn't have the time and energy. The LinkedIn newsfeed will in the future be less likely to show you posts from this person with this type of wording or text. The result? The next time you access LinkedIn, your feed has become that little bit more of a congratulatory merry-go-round, where the only posts you see on the newsfeed are people with success.

The outcome of this is a kind of fake LinkedIn universe, where everyone is happy, working, interested, and committed to "groundbreaking" science and winning grants. The LinkedIn algorithm has inadvertently made you complicit in this "success feed" even if you actively fought it.

A kind and ethical approach would be to consciously avoid bragging about your successes, so that you do not contribute to this. This is *really* difficult for most of us and brings along its own set of problems. How can you, after all, *not* let your network know about it if what you have been striving for is achieved? Say you have just got your work published. The key staff member in a research foundation who follows you would be delighted to know that your work has been published. Your scientific peers *need* to know if their scientific work can use your work as a stepping stone for their own research.

But what we *can* do is to consciously fight the platforms' bias for success by truthfully sharing our failures and disappointments also. You can share the "dark side" that is often embedded in ultimate success. And you can deliberately encourage others to share their vulnerabilities by making an effort to show your appreciation with a comment (or whatever emoji is appropriate) when they do so.

Shifting to a kind mindset

We believe that the value of kindness and generosity should be an integral part of our professional lives, and that our kind and generous actions make for better science and a better society.

To this end, scientists have a responsibility to ensure that their interactions on social media reflect this value.

Let us look now at the networking function (see Table 2.1) on social media in terms of this kindness ethic. Meeting scholars in your own field, and people who work in related areas, gives you access to better opportunities. That is, after all, one of the reasons why you use social media: to meet new people with whom you can work. Highly networked people tend to float to the top and gain status (Lin, 2001).

But what about your peers' and colleagues' networks?

Social media let you link up others, that is forge links between people who both know you individually, but not each other. The sociological term for this is triadic closure (Rapoport, 1953): if you are the link that two people have in common, they are more likely to be linked at some point in the future, not just because they both know you, but because they are likely to share interests, location, and profession or field. You can help this along the way by getting people in contact with each other for specific reasons.

From an ethical standpoint, forging connections between two people who are not aware of each other is *for their sake*, not yours. Maybe there is a research or course opportunity that you think another person should be aware of. Maybe the two people you know share a common interest. Either way, the generous thing is to make them aware of each other's existence. Social media deliver both the framework and the occasion for this kind of triadic closure. They let it happen, and they give us an excuse for doing so.

An example of this is how people on LinkedIn will see a job opportunity on their newsfeed and simply tag someone they know in the comment field to let them know. So, LinkedIn is the enabler of this triadic closure between the person posting about the job, you, and the person whom you think will be interested in it. But it also gives us a low-effort excuse and occasion to renew our connection to the two people with whom we have connected.

This is an example of what we believe researchers should do more of, and something that can enable a shift to a kind mindset.

Ever since the first of the currently operating social media platforms came about with LinkedIn in 2003 and Twitter (now X) in 2006, the prevailing culture for researchers has been to use social media as a means for scientists to boost themselves and their own work, and to somehow win the networking game. But by shifting to a kind mindset, you can help create a culture change, where the purpose and aim is for your actions to have a positive effect on others.

We believe that a shift to this mindset is ultimately more rewarding and can serve as an antidote to a stressful and, ultimately, unproductive research culture where everyone is attempting to boost their own research to the detriment of everyone else. In other words, it allows moving from a zero-sum to a positive-sum game.

How to be kind: Practical social media ideas for researchers

By consciously cultivating a culture of kindness and generosity in our online interactions, we can ensure that the social media research community remains a space where ideas are shared, critiques are constructive, and connections are genuine.

We believe that being kind in our social media interactions is not just about being a good person. It helps the advancement of science. By treating other scientists on social media with kindness, we can better foster innovation, ideation, and intellectual growth in the academic community.

In the following, we list a few practical ways to be kind and generous on social media.

Share with gratitude

When you share your findings, express your gratitude to that select group of people who have made it possible, and who may not be mentioned as co-authors. Your research will always build on the work of countless others, and your findings might serve as the foundation for future discoveries and uses by others invisible to you. By taking this into account when you share your work, you are paying forward the generosity of those who came before you.

Just as an example, you might want to publicly thank an early career mentor for their early support for an idea that led to the project and paper that you link to on the LinkedIn platform: "I couldn't have completed this without the guidance of @MentorName—you started me on this path, and your insights were invaluable!"

Be open about doubts, concerns, and details

Revealing your own data and methods can be scary on social media, especially if you—like many of us—have doubts about the real excellence of your work. You might worry that this openness could expose you to criticism or that someone might "scoop" your work.

We may, indeed, need space for our own reflection, and feedback from a smaller group, before we are willing to share our research.

But often our fears are unfounded. And when you share, you invite collaboration, encourage replication, and help others to build on your work from an earlier stage in the research process.

One way to do this is to maintain an open blog, either on your own website or on a page hosted by others or your institution, where you openly summarise and discuss any challenges or uncertainties you faced during your research. Then regularly post links to this blog at each new stage in the research process. The post could be something like this:

> During our study on Y, we encountered some unexpected results that we're still trying to understand. We initially hypothesized A, but our data suggested something different. If anyone has insights or has faced similar issues, I'd love to hear your thoughts.

Amplify others' work, even if it is "competing"

It might seem counterintuitive to promote others when you are striving for your own recognition within a given field. But when you retweet a colleague's paper, even a colleague who is doing "competing" work close to your own project and expertise, you are contributing to a more supportive scientific community.

This is particularly important if you are a senior scientist and already have status and name recognition in your field. Social media platforms can dramatically increase the impact of younger scientists who have not yet gained the same reach as you.

Being kind and amplifying others' work on social media, especially if you perceive them as competitors, can be difficult for us. But, if this is what you need, here is an egotistical reason for it: by sharing your competitors' work, you are effectively signalling to interested third parties that you precisely do *not* perceive them as a competitor. This also works as a cognitive trick to play on yourself! By sharing competitors' work, they cease to be a competitor in your mind.

It could go like this: repost a colleague's publication announcement on X with a comment like, "Don't miss this important paper on [subject] by @ColleagueName—great contribution to our understanding of [this phenomenon]!"

Post about your failures

Share your challenges, failed experiments, and rejections. This doesn't mean that you should wallow in negativity, but rather provide a balanced view of what it means to be a scientist. Your authenticity can help demystify the process for others, particularly early career scientists who might feel isolated in their struggles.

Post about a failed experiment or a rejected grant proposal on LinkedIn, sharing what you learned from the experience. For example, "While this grant didn't go through, the feedback was invaluable and has strengthened my future proposals. Happy to discuss if anyone's interested in what I learned."

An alternative is to share it without saying what you learned from the experience. In some ways, this is better, as it does not presume that failure is actually "success": "I just received word that my grant application for [project] wasn't successful. Right now, it's a tough pill to swallow".

Be the go-between

By introducing your connections to others who might benefit from knowing each other—triadic closure—you can actively help others with absolutely no self-promotion involved. Indeed, by enabling this brokering function, social media platforms work to help the research community, and also society in general.

Putting specific people together on social media should be valuable to both parties. Maybe there is a job, a research collaboration opportunity, or a course offering that you think another person should be aware of. Maybe the two people just share a common interest.

Social media platforms have different tagging technologies to enable this. All of them involve using the "@" sign in the comment field and adding the name or account of the person who needs to be tagged. They are different, however, in terms of how easy they can get the person's account to populate. On LinkedIn, it is relatively simple: all you have to do is write "@" and add their name in the comment field after a post that is relevant to them. Most of the time, LinkedIn will populate it as a tag (if the person has a LinkedIn account) that you will see marked in bold, and they will receive a notification. If the name does not populate, you can try with a "-" dash or "_" between the first and last name.

Being an intermediary can also be via direct message. If you are connected to a person on LinkedIn, you can write a direct LinkedIn message to them: "Hey [name], I came across this job opening for a pharmaceutical scientist at [Company Name]. It seems like a great fit, especially with your experience with [specific skill or project]. You'd be a strong candidate".

Another great way to introduce two people in your network who might benefit from knowing each other is a method that we believe could be used more often. You could write directly in the comment field of a LinkedIn post, or as a reply to an X or Bluesky post: "@[Person1], meet @[Person2]—both of you are doing fantastic work on [subject] and might find some great synergies!"

Like all good brokering actions, this allow the two parties to decide for themselves how or whether to proceed.

Respond thoughtfully to posts that have few responses

It can be tempting to react immediately to a post, particularly if it challenges your views or status, or if you perceive it as an encroachment on your position in a field.

Say, for the sake of argument, that you wanted to ensure that you are the most dominant player in a specific research field on social media. You could, in theory, set up a complete routine to safeguard this position, by monitoring keywords as we explained in Chapter 6 and responding to every post on social media that has anything to do with your field as a way to showcase your own dominance. But this is profoundly unethical.

And you can consciously avoid this.

Take a moment to think before you respond. Is your comment adding value to the conversation beyond what has already been said? Are you respecting the original poster's perspective, even if you disagree? A rushed or poorly considered reply can discourage someone from sharing their ideas in the future.

You can even go further. Let us try something radically new! You can, as an exercise, *only* reply to posts that have not set off a discussion already and that have not been started by someone in your current network. This will not only allow you to meet new people in your field and gain new insights, but you can also avoid only reacting to what the social media algorithms deem to be popular.

Social media platforms are designed to amplify those with the "loudest" voices, and they then dominate the newsfeeds as a result. Using the above routine forces you to listen to those softer voices who are either not represented at all or who are drowned out by the heavy hitters. This isn't just a nice thing to do—you can also see it as an ethical responsibility.

This is one of the ways you can do it in practice. Set up a bookmarked LinkedIn search with keywords related to your field (see Chapter 6), such as "neuroscience research" or "open innovation", and filter for your location or university. This search will act as an alternative newsfeed, bringing up posts and discussions from early career scientists who are not yet prominent in your network and who have not been fed to you by the LinkedIn algorithm. Regularly and thoughtfully comment on the posts that are valuable, but that have not set off a discussion.

Promote slowness

The pull of the new, the pressure of novelty on social media platforms is designed to give us a sense of vertigo. But this can lead to stress on the platforms used by scientists: if you don't follow your field on a day-to-day basis, you are somehow "behind".

You can consciously fight this sense of urgency. One method is to have a routine of reposting older, yet still relevant, content from your network. You thereby push back against the underlying premise of social media in science—that it is the place to be updated on the "latest".

How can you do this? You can deliberately repost posts from your network that are NOT the latest ones showing up on your feed. This could be something that is still relevant, but that was posted a week, month, or year ago. A "throwback" science routine like this would resurface valuable older posts from others. You can find them by setting up a bookmarked search (see Chapter 6) and deliberately scrolling past a certain time frame. Give it a name like "Throwback Science" or "Timeless Insights". Credit the original poster and express appreciation for their contribution in the post. Then ask open-ended questions like, "How have your views on x evolved since this was originally posted?"

Always assume good intentions, and trust in others' comprehension

By deliberately assuming that others are debating in good faith, scientists can foster a more constructive and respectful dialogue. This is particularly relevant in science because discussions often involve complex, nuanced topics where misunderstandings can easily arise.

Take this example. Someone has posted about your just-released paper on Bluesky or another microblogging platform like X with the following text: "Interesting paper on climate modelling, but I think the authors overlooked some key variables in their analysis".

You may be inclined to reply to this post with the following: "Clearly, you didn't read the methodology section properly. The variables you're talking about were accounted for". However, by responding with the assumption of good intent, you can invite the original poster to become your ally in getting to the bottom of the problem: "Thanks for pointing that out! It's a complex area—could you elaborate on which variables you think were missed? I'd love to understand your perspective".

This response forces the original poster to enter into a serious dialogue with your work and be more specific. It has the added benefit that if they then do not respond, you have found out that their criticism was not in good faith (see also Box 8.5 for our Reflective Response Framework and Box 8.6 on "sealioning").

This brings us on to a second point. It is kind and generous to respect your interlocutor's intelligence and engage in real dialogue, even if you (secretly) suspect that they will find it difficult to grasp what you say.

It can be difficult, but when you respond to questions or comments, you should consciously approach them as an opportunity for dialogue rather than a one-way teaching moment or as a means to position yourself as a thought leader within your field.

Resist the urge to dominate the conversation. Your goal should be to foster understanding, also your own understanding, not to "win" an argument. This approach is not only kinder but also contributes to a healthier, more productive, and more intellectually stimulating scientific discourse.

Be true

The last point in our list of practical ways to be kind and generous as a scientist is to be truthful and to never exaggerate the implications of your research.

This can be difficult in a prevailing university culture of promoting "innovative" research. But as individual scientists, being kind means that you don't invite anyone to read something that you honestly don't think they will be interested in. In other words, this means no clickbait. And it means not using a word like "groundbreaking" in any post—unless, of course, it is about drilling holes in the ground!

A thread on X, for example, can start with a caveat: "This new paper on [subject] has some interesting findings, but keep in mind the small sample size. Worth discussing!"

The long-term impact of kindness

If you, as we do, mostly follow scientists on social media, it can be a depressing experience to scroll through your newsfeed. You get the impression that scientists communicate with others on social media fundamentally to promote themselves and their careers.

This is the logic of marketing, where social media success is only measured in altmetrics (see Chapter 2), research paper download numbers, citations, and prestige. With that logic, social media activity is about fighting for space in a zero-sum attention economy rather than the positive-sum goal of developing your own thinking or your broader field.

Some academics, prone to even more strategic thinking, strive to achieve "thought leadership" using techniques from the world of lobbying to dominate the social media debate on a particular topic. For them, it is not about cultivating opposing views but about winning and owning their position in the research space.

However, we believe that social media should be in the service of science, society, humanity, thought, and well-being. These obligations are, by their nature, *difficult*.

It can feel hard to have the energy to promote others when you are also striving for your own recognition in a competitive academia. But remember that it is not just about you. And small, kind actions online can lead to significant, long-term changes in the academic world.

We believe that at its best, social media can be something noble, something human. Social media have been referred to as the "global computer in the cloud" (Rao, 2019), allowing something analogous to a collective thought process to emerge out of all the myriad interactions. It arguably speeds up and improves the collective scientific endeavour.

But to make this happen, you have to be willing to stop using social media only strategically, and to start communicating with authenticity, kindness, generosity, and honesty.

10

STRATEGY

From reflection to action

> I've always been someone who tries to convert any sort of opportunity into something that is concrete and impactful.
> —Krithika Randhawa, Associate Professor
> at the University of Sydney

A framework for goal-driven social media platform interaction

Throughout this book, we have explored how social media can transform your research communication, expand your scholarly networks, and enhance the impact of your academic work. We have examined specific platforms and discussed best practices for profiles, posts, visuals, filtering, automation, and AI augmentation. We have confronted the darker aspects of social media and encouraged the lighter aspects that will reinforce a kinder and more generous academic culture. Now we will explore how you can turn this understanding into action.

We urge all researchers to develop their social media presence. For us, "to be or not to be on social media" is not an existential question that is worth asking. The real question is *how* you connect with others on social media, and what forms of dialogue and collaboration on the platforms will deliver the most value to you, your discipline, and society. There is no single, universal path for you to follow. Your social media strategy should reflect your specific situation and will depend on factors such as your discipline, career stage, institutional environment, and even geopolitical conditions.

To this end, we offer a framework to develop your social media strategy that can adapt to the shifting mix of platforms and tools. Given the complexity and contextual nature of academic social media interactions, our framework offers a structure to help you make decisions about your approach. We call this the Researcher's Social Media

DOI: 10.4324/9781003589341-10

Compass, building on principles first outlined in Bogers (2021) and expanded here. See Box 10.1 for what this could mean in practice.

BOX 10.1: FINDING YOUR OWN WAY

There is no single right way to "do" social media for research impact. Your approach will depend on your goals, your field, your timing—and as innovation researcher *Krithika Randhawa, Associate Professor at the University of Sydney*, found out—your readiness to embrace some messiness along the way.

"It's been very much an experiment", she explains, adding that she made up her strategy as she went along. Just like in our Researcher's Social Media Compass (see the section "The researcher's social media compass" in this chapter)—each dimension of her activity evolved organically.

Krithika started by using social media to just explore emerging phenomena on her feeds and send connection requests to like-minded researchers. Over time, she expanded her approach to include posting visuals, talking to practitioners related to her field, and taking part in broader public conversations online. The key shift for her was learning to frame her posts differently. She no longer simply promoted her work, but strove with her posts to create "a conversation around a key theme", as she explains.

When she posted about industrial platform ecosystems, she said practitioners didn't just read the post and move on, but they adapted her framework to their own contexts. And this, in turn, allowed more fortunate things to happen. A government agency discovered her work online and invited her to speak at a national policy event. A consultant found her through LinkedIn, which sparked an ongoing chain of collaborations, podcast appearances, course materials, and new grant ideas.

"I've always been someone who tries to convert any sort of opportunity into something that is concrete and impactful", she reflects. 'Serendipity' (see Box 3.3) was enabled by maintaining a consistent presence and being willing to follow up on unexpected connections.

The Researcher's Social Media Compass

As we have established in this book, social media are an essential tool for academics seeking to enhance their research impact, build networks, and interact with their diverse stakeholders. However, navigating these digital spaces demands a thoughtful, strategic approach aligned with both scholarly goals and personal values.

Drawing on research in knowledge sharing (Leonardi, 2014), scholarly communication (Carrigan, 2019), and academic identity (Costa, 2013), we propose the Researcher's Social Media Compass to help researchers develop effective social media strategies. This framework integrates insights from studies of digital scholarly practices (Weller, 2011) with research on open innovation and knowledge exchange (Bogers et al., 2017).

At the centre of the framework is *Purpose*—your "core" or fundamental motivations for interacting through social media. Surrounding this core are four interconnected dimensions: *Presence* (your digital identity), *Platform* (your chosen tools), *Personality* (your authentic voice), and *Practice* (your sustainable routines). Figure 10.1 is a visual representation.

As Veletsianos and Kimmons (2012) argue, networked participation in academic contexts involves complex negotiations between

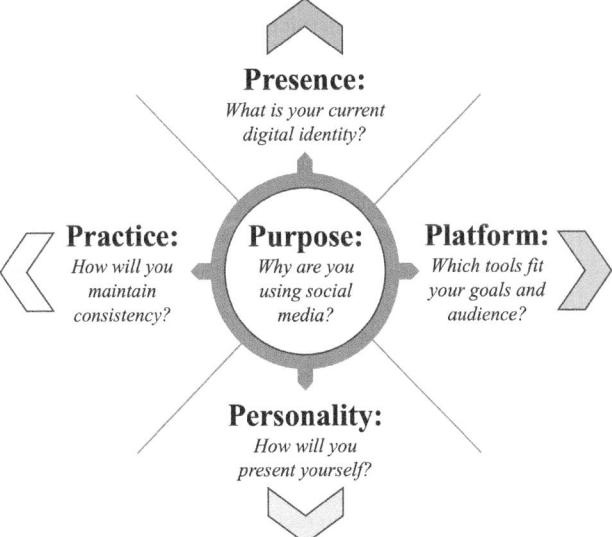

FIGURE 10.1 The Researcher's Social Media Compass.

professional norms, personal identity, and technological affordances. The Researcher's Social Media Compass acknowledges these complexities while providing practical guidance for academics at any career stage.

In this book, we have already explored each of these dimensions individually, highlighting strategies and examples drawn from successful social media practitioners in academia. In Chapter 2, we presented the "Purpose" dimension and mapped out why academics use social media for research impact in our Reflective Model of Scientists' Social Media Use. In Chapter 3, we presented the "Platform" dimension and offered an overview of which social media platforms do what. In Chapter 4, we looked at "Presence" and how your public-facing user profiles help to define yourself professionally. In Chapters 5–7, we offered guidance for the "Practice" dimension in the form of posts, curating feeds, and automation. And finally, in Chapters 8 and 9, we looked at the "Personality" dimension, both in terms of the dark and the bright sides of academic social media. Our approach recognises that effective social media interactions don't maximise metrics, but rather thoughtfully aligns your online presence with your scholarly goals and values (Greenhow & Gleason, 2014).

Whether you're new to social media or looking to refine your existing approach, the Researcher's Social Media Compass offers a structured way to develop a sustainable, authentic, and impactful digital presence that enhances rather than detracts from your academic work.

Let us examine each of these dimensions in more detail.

Purpose: Clarifying your "why"

Clear purpose is the foundation of effective scholarly social media use. Without it, your presence can become scattered, ineffective, or unsustainable. When you set out explicit goals for your social media use, you will experience higher satisfaction and perceived impact than when you use the platforms aimlessly.

Start by asking yourself: what do I want to achieve through my social media exchanges? As we established in Chapter 2, academics may have a variety of objectives to achieve through their social media use. Common goals for academics include disseminating research findings to reach more readers and potential citers, building a professional network of collaborators and colleagues, advancing public understanding of your field or research area, interacting with people outside academia who might apply your work, learning from others by curating information sources and participating in discussions, and developing ideas through dialogue with peers and potential collaborators. These goals aren't mutually exclusive, but prioritising helps you make decisions about where and how to invest your limited time and attention.

Your purpose should inform who you aim to reach. Are you primarily communicating with other academics in your specific field, scholars from adjacent disciplines, students and early career researchers, policymakers or practitioners, media professionals, or the general public? Different audiences require different platforms, content approaches, and interaction styles (see Chapters 3–5).

Finally, defining success metrics aligned with your purpose helps evaluate whether your efforts are worthwhile. These might include quantitative measures such as followers, citations, and reach, or qualitative outcomes like quality of connections, new collaborations, and policy influence. By now, you will be aware of our scepticism towards quantitative metrics like followers, citations, and reach. But clarifying these metrics in advance can help maintain your own focus if this keeps you on the straight and narrow.

Presence: Assessing your digital identity

Your digital presence extends beyond social media to include your entire online footprint. Before expanding this digital presence, take stock of what already exists. Google yourself as others would and consider what information about you is already publicly available. Do the top search results accurately reflect your current work and interests? Are there gaps, outdated information, or misrepresentations? How discoverable are you to those who might want to find your work?

This audit forms the baseline for your strategy. If you're already highly visible but with outdated or misrepresentative content, your approach might focus on updating and curating. If you're relatively invisible online, you may need to build foundational elements like professional profiles and research identifiers (e.g., ORCID). If you have a clear and coherent digital identity, you are more likely to be found by potential collaborators and cited by peers.

For most academics, a minimal effective presence includes a current institutional profile page with key information, consistent profiles on scholarly platforms like Google Scholar, at least one professional social media profile on a platform where your research community already exists, and clear identification and links between these various presences whose interconnected elements enhance your visibility and reputation.

Platform: Making strategic choices

Platform selection should flow from your purpose and target audiences. As we explored in Chapter 3, each platform has distinct characteristics that make it more or less suitable for your particular goals.

When evaluating platforms, consider where your intended audience is active, which varies by discipline, geography, and professional sector. Think about what types of content and interaction the platform supports—some are better for long-form posts, others for quick interactions, still others for visual communication. Assess how much control you have over your data and connections, including data ownership, portability, and platform stability. Be realistic about the time investment required to use the platform effectively, as some platforms demand frequent, regular posting to maintain your visibility. Finally, consider how the platform aligns with your personal and institutional values, including governance, moderation policies, and data practices.

Rather than trying to maintain a presence everywhere, most academics benefit from a focused approach. A tiered strategy works best: one or two primary platforms where you invest most of your social media time and energy, with a small number of secondary platforms where you maintain basic profiles and occasionally contribute, and potentially a few experimental spaces where you can explore new platforms with low commitment. This tiered approach allows you to concentrate your efforts where they matter most while remaining open to emerging opportunities. And by knowing what you want to focus on, you can also let go of those things that are outside that scope—there is only so much you can do.

There are differences in reach and number of interactions across platforms, with some allowing much more public exposure than others. Your selection should be influenced by whether you're primarily seeking interactions with peers, the public, or other stakeholders.

Personality: Finding your authentic voice

How you present yourself online—your tone of voice, level of personal disclosure, style of interaction, and choices about what you post—collectively constitute your digital personality. Research on academic social media effectiveness consistently highlights authenticity as a key factor in building genuine connections (see also Chapter 5).

Finding your authentic voice means balancing professional and personal dimensions—how much of your non-academic life do you want to share? This varies tremendously among successful academic social media users. Academic writing often values formality, but social media generally reward more conversational approaches. You'll need to navigate depth and accessibility, translating complex ideas for audiences with different domain expertise, without oversimplifying, and this requires skill and practice. Finally, as we discussed in Chapter 8, you should weigh advocacy and neutrality—how vocal do you want to be about political or controversial issues related to your work?

What matters is finding an approach that feels authentic to you, serves your purposes, and can be sustained over time. Effective academic identities on social media aren't simply translations of offline personas. They are thoughtful constructions that remain true to core scholarly values while adapting to digital contexts (Fransman, 2013).

Setting clear personal boundaries is important. It may not be possible to decide in advance, but it helps to think about what topics are off-limits for discussion, how you'll respond to criticism or disagreement, when you'll engage in debate and when you'll step back, and how you'll handle requests for time or attention. These boundaries will protect your well-being and help maintain consistency in your online presence. Marwick and boyd (2011) describe this as "context collapse management"—the strategies people employ to navigate different audiences in shared digital spaces.

Practice: Developing sustainable routines

Even the most perfectly conceived social media strategy will fail when it's not sustained. Routines need to be manageable if they are to be successful in the long run.

In Chapter 6, we outlined a process for thoughtful time management, designating specific times for social media platforms rather than letting them fragment your attention throughout the day. In this system, the planning of posts is important—developing systems to capture ideas and prepare content in batches, when possible, helps maintain consistency. Finding a sustainable rhythm, a cadence of posting and interaction that suits your schedule and platform norms, will help prevent burnout. Appropriate tools and automation can streamline routine tasks without losing authenticity (as discussed in Chapter 7). Finally, a regular evaluation of what works and what doesn't allow you to adjust and refine your approach.

These practices should align with your broader work habits and preferences. As we outlined in Chapter 6, some will prefer to integrate social media into their daily workflow, while others will dedicate specific "social media days" or blocks of time. But as we described, creating a workflow that has clear boundaries around your social media use will increase your productivity and satisfaction compared to if you allow it to permeate your entire workday. In the end, we suggest creating routines that allow you to harness digital tools' benefits while protecting the cognitive resources needed for other deep scholarly work. This might include designated device-free times, social media "sabbaticals", or technological aids that limit distractions.

Framework integration: Creating your personal strategy

The five Ps in the Researcher's Social Media Compass—Purpose, Presence, Platform, Personality, and Practice—work in concert to create a coherent social media approach for scholars (see Figure 10.1 for an overview). The effectiveness of your strategy depends not only on how well you address each dimension individually, but also specifically on how they align with and reinforce one another.

For instance, your Purpose (disseminating research to policymakers) should direct your Platform choices (perhaps LinkedIn or X), which in turn will influence your Personality (professional but accessible) and Practice (timed around policy cycles and events). Misalignments between these elements create friction—an ambitious Purpose without matching Practice routines will lead to frustration, while a well-developed Presence on Platforms your target audience doesn't use will be wasted effort. Ultimately, both your own satisfaction and impact will be best achieved by aligning what you want to achieve, where you interact, how you present yourself, and the routines you develop to sustain your efforts.

Table 10.1 offers key questions to consider along the five dimensions of the Researcher's Social Media Compass framework. Creating your personal strategy involves working through these questions and identifying the interconnections between your answers. This isn't a one-time exercise because effective social media strategies evolve as your career develops, as platforms change, and as you learn what works best for your specific context.

TABLE 10.1 Key Questions in the Researcher's Social Media Compass

Purpose	What are my primary goals for social media use?
	Who am I specifically trying to reach?
	How will I measure success?
	How does this align with my broader research and career goals?
Presence	What is my current digital footprint?
	What impression does my online presence create?
	What gaps or inconsistencies exist?
	What level of visibility is appropriate for my career stage and goals?
Platform	Where are my target audiences active?
	Which platforms support the type of content that I want to share, and interactions that I want?
	What is the time investment required for each platform?
	How stable and aligned with my values are these platforms?
Personality	What balance of professional and personal sharing feels authentic to me?
	How formal or conversational should my tone be?
	What boundaries will I set around topics and interactions?
	How will I handle disagreement or criticism?
Practice	What specific times will I dedicate to social media?
	How will I keep track of ideas from the platform and plan my own posts?
	What tools might help me maintain consistency?
	How often will I review and adjust my approach?
	How will I protect time for deep work?

As McCarthy and Bogers (2023) argue in their article on the "open academic", social media strategy should be viewed as a dynamic capability that scholars develop over time, not as a static plan. Regular reflection on how well your current approach serves your evolving goals is essential for long-term effectiveness and sustainability.

11

CONCLUSION

Navigating a dynamic social media landscape

> We are making the community visible to itself.
> —Aleksi Aaltonen, Associate Professor at
> the Stevens Institute of Technology

The future lies in your hands: How to make it happen

As we approach the end of the book, we shift the focus towards the future. We discuss implications for scholars and other stakeholders, review some key trends, and discuss how you can manage and balance the trade-offs.

Let us start with individual academics like you, the person whom we primarily have addressed in this book. Several strategic approaches can enhance your social media effectiveness while minimising potential drawbacks.

Starting small but purposeful is crucial. Begin with a focused presence on one platform where your community is active, rather than trying to be everywhere at once. This allows you to develop your fluency on one platform and build meaningful connections before expanding your digital footprint. Many successful academic social media users began with a single platform that aligned well with their field's communication preferences.

Align how you interact on the platforms with how you currently do research. This will yield more sustainable results than if you set up a separate track of social media activity. Use social media to amplify work that you're already doing, and think of it as a dimension within your scholarly work rather than an additional burden. You can share updates about your ongoing projects, highlight your own recently published papers, or discuss conferences and events related to your research interests. But note also that you don't necessarily have to post

DOI: 10.4324/9781003589341-11

only about *your* work. It's just as valuable—if not more so—to relate to others' work. You may also simply react to others' posts.

Building your digital skills incrementally will prevent you from being overwhelmed. Focus on developing one new skill each semester or year—it could be, say, infographics, brief writing, video, or podcast creation. Each of these skills will equip you with new ways to share ideas, meet new people, and co-create. A gradual approach will let you expand your capabilities without disrupting your primary research and teaching responsibilities.

Documenting your impact is essential in an academic setting that increasingly values public outreach but may not have the formal methods to assess it. Keep records of significant outcomes from your social media interactions, such as new collaborations, media coverage, policy influence, or community partnerships. These records can provide valuable evidence for promotion and tenure committees.

Finding your community on social media platforms can provide mutual support and amplification. Identify and connect with others who share similar approaches or interests in your field. These connections often lead to informal mentoring relationships, collaborative opportunities, and expanded networks that extend beyond digital spaces into conference meetings and research partnerships.

Being explicit about boundaries helps manage expectations and protect your time. Signal to followers when you're available for dialogue and when you're focusing elsewhere. Some academics use status updates to indicate when they're on social media "sabbaticals" during intensive writing periods or create standard responses for common requests.

The key is to develop an approach that enhances rather than detracts from your core scholarly work and personal well-being. Social media should serve your academic goals, not compete with them.

Your wider social media ecosystem

This book is written as a practical guide for you as a scholar, but it has implications for multiple stakeholders as part of your wider stakeholder ecosystem.

Research groups and departments

At the department and research group level, coordination of social media activity offers significant advantages over individual efforts working in isolation.

Coordinating rather than duplicating efforts allows team members to develop complementary roles and approaches. Not everyone needs to maintain the same level of social media presence. Some might focus on creating posts, others on network building, and still others on responding to mentions and requests. This division of labour can make the collective social media presence more sustainable and effective than if everyone is attempting to do everything.

Institutional accounts or pages that represent larger institutions are outside the scope of this book. But on a smaller scale, "curation rotations", where researchers take turns to post from a research group account, are a great way to bring in new voices and relieve some of the burden.

Creating shared resources enhances efficiency. Departments and research groups can build common visuals, messaging templates, and content repositories that team members can draw upon, including, for example, department logos, standard descriptions of research areas, high-quality images of laboratory facilities, or templates for disseminating recent publications. The startup effort for individuals beginning their social media activity is consequently reduced.

Setting up a mentoring structure can pair digitally experienced members with those who are developing skills to facilitate knowledge transfer. This approach benefits both parties—newer users gain practical guidance while experienced communicators often find that teaching others clarifies their own thinking and practices. These mentoring relationships can be formal arrangements or ad hoc arrangements based on specific needs.

Recognising diverse contributions acknowledges that team members will have different strengths and preferences in digital outreach. Some may excel at creating visual explanations, others at writing accessible summaries of complex research, and still others at building relationships with non-academic stakeholders. Valuing these different contributions leads to a more inclusive participatory environment.

If you are responsible for a research group or department level social media co-operation, you should establish explicit expectations about social media participation to prevent misunderstandings and reduce anxiety. Researchers need clarity about which activities are required rather than optional, and how social media involvement fits into workload considerations. Transparent policies about representing the department or research group also help members understand when they should speak as individuals as opposed to when they are representing the institution.

By sharing examples of impact achieved through social media participation, you can motivate continued efforts by your colleagues, by demonstrating tangible benefits, and by providing concrete models that others can adapt to their own work. Celebrating these successes in department meetings or newsletters reinforces the value placed on effective communication.

External communities or organisations, including interest groups or conferences that your research group is a part of, can also complement or even replace your own social media work here.

To sum up, departments and research groups that take a strategic approach to social media can enhance their collective visibility while distributing the workload sustainably across members with different capabilities and interests.

University communicators

For institutional communication professionals at department, faculty, and university levels, the evolving social media landscape requires new approaches to academic support. University communicators play a crucial role in creating environments where researchers can have societal impact via social media with minimal risk while maximising institutional and individual benefits. But we believe that institutions are best served by shifting from control to empowerment. This means moving beyond top-down messaging to providing researchers with the tools, training, and platforms to tell their own stories. This doesn't mean abandoning institutional messaging. It means complementing it with authentic voices from the research community. Communication professionals can develop frameworks and guidance that help academics communicate effectively while maintaining their distinctive perspectives.

If you are a communications professional at a university, you should target your support to the research areas and individuals where it can have the greatest impact. With limited resources, trying to support everyone equally often results in helping no one effectively. Communication teams might focus on "brand ambassadors" by offering social media training to scientists who have already shown motivation and activity on social media. Or they might focus on research projects with significant public interest, projects approaching major milestones, or the areas aligned with institutional priorities. This focused approach generates examples that can then inspire broader participation.

Developing clear crisis protocols creates guidelines for managing negative attention or controversies that may arise from public activity, including social media storms. Researchers may face sudden attention, backlash, or misrepresentation online, and universities need plans in place to support them. These protocols should outline escalation procedures, designate spokesperson roles, and provide templates for responses to common scenarios. Having these resources ready before they're needed reduces stress and improves response quality when challenges arise.

Measuring what matters involves developing impact metrics that capture meaningful outcomes beyond simple reach or impression counts. These might include policy citations, community partnerships formed, student recruitment influenced by social media activity, or funding opportunities that emerge from increased visibility. These substantive metrics help demonstrate the value of communication investments.

Advocating internally for recognition of online public activity, including social media activity, in promotion and tenure processes, and for resources to support these activities, helps create an institutional environment where these activities are valued rather than merely expected. Communication professionals can help academic leadership understand the strategic importance of online engagements with other stakeholders and the public, and the resources required to do it effectively.

Policy and funding bodies

For research funders and policy organisations, decisions about how to support and evaluate communication, including professional social media activity, have wider impacts on how academics are active.

Aligning incentives with expectations is fundamental. If sharing and interacting online is expected of researchers, it should be funded, trained for, and recognised in evaluation criteria. Too often, these activities are mandated without corresponding resources or recognition, creating unsustainable pressures on researchers. Integrated approaches that fund communication activities as part of research grants and recognise social media and traditional media activity in evaluations create more viable systems.

Funding communication infrastructure supports the development of platforms, tools, and training that enhance researchers' ability to communicate effectively. This might include support for open-access publication platforms, visualisation tools designed for scientific communication, or training programmes that build researchers' digital communication and social media skills. These infrastructure investments can benefit entire research communities rather than individual projects.

Balancing speed with accuracy is a central challenge for researchers engaging in fast-moving policy debates. Social media platforms have become informal but powerful arenas where scientists can offer timely insights—often in response to emerging crises or unfolding events. Funders and policy bodies should create mechanisms that allow researchers to contribute to time-sensitive discussions while maintaining scientific integrity. This could include formally acknowledging social media contributions in funding assessments and providing training in real-time science communication.

Fostering cross-disciplinary communication increasingly means helping researchers connect and collaborate across fields on social media. Many societal challenges require insights from multiple disciplines, but academic silos can impede effective collaboration. Programmes that specifically support interdisciplinary communication help bridge these divides.

Supporting vulnerable communicators means helping early career researchers and those from underrepresented groups interact with others safely and effectively on social media. These researchers often have the most to gain from increased visibility, but they also face disproportionate risks. Targeted support might include specialised training, financial support for communication activities, or mentoring programmes that connect them with experienced communicators in their fields.

Policy and funding bodies should expand the definition of research impact to include various forms of public engagement, including social media activity and influence. Traditional metrics focused on academic citations capture only a fraction of the ways research creates value. Broader frameworks that acknowledge contributions to policy, practice, public discourse, and cultural understanding provide a more complete picture.

Organisations that determine policy and funding have the power to shape the ecosystem in which academic communication occurs. Their decisions influence not only what gets communicated, but also who participates in these activities, and how they're valued within academic institutions.

What's changing in researchers' use of social media

Researchers' social media practices are changing rapidly. Just a few years ago, Twitter (now X) was a dominant platform across disciplines. Today, we see migrations and dispersions across multiple platforms, including Bluesky, Mastodon, LinkedIn, and, as we have listed examples of in Tables 3.1–3.5, a host of minor platforms that have value for specific fields, audiences, and practices. This fragmentation creates both challenges and opportunities for scholars seeking to establish a meaningful way to be seen, to meet, to be inspired, and to collaborate online.

In Chapter 3, we introduced the distinction between the social graph and the interest graph. The social graph is the logic behind platforms like Facebook, which connects people who have a shared history, typically colleagues, friends, family, and close acquaintances. It's built on existing relationships and often reinforces what are called strong ties.

By contrast, the interest graph, which Twitter pioneered, connects people based on shared interests and topics, regardless of prior relationships. It thereby often enables weak ties across geographic and disciplinary boundaries, making it particularly valuable for researchers seeking diverse perspectives.

Research on academic social networks confirms the power of weak ties for innovation and impact. As Granovetter's (1973) seminal work demonstrated, weak ties serve as bridges between otherwise disconnected social clusters, providing access to novel information and opportunities. In the academic context, these weak ties are often where the most fruitful collaborations begin.

The platforms that have emerged in recent years, and that have been taken up by academics, have features that strike a new balance between these two principles, but are weighted towards the interest graph. They accentuate the interest rather than the social graph, thereby letting you forge weak ties to other scholars in multiple and separate niche communities. Bluesky, for example, lets users customise feeds to an extraordinary degree, allowing you to heavily curate your own experience based on topics rather than simply following people. Mastodon's instance-based structure has pioneered separate communities of interest, each with their own rules and moderation, but with cross-instance discovery. LinkedIn, which originally primarily enabled "social graph" connections to colleagues in a work setting, has in recent years moved to an "interest graph" logic that allows weaker ties based on niche interests. In Box 11.1, there is an example of how a community has arisen around a niche interest or research field as a result of social media activity.

BOX 11.1: DATA STUDIES WAKES UP AND SEES ITSELF

The two scholars had long sensed there was a shared interest in their research community, but there was no central place where the researchers could find each other. So, they decided to create one via a social media routine.

Associate Professor Aleksi Aaltonen of the Stevens Institute of Technology and *Assistant Professor Marta Stelmaszak Rosa of the University of Massachusetts Amherst* share a research focus on data studies in management and information systems. They needed a way to make the field visible—and social.

First, they created a website that featured nearly 100 carefully selected papers from top journals in their field; then they took to LinkedIn. Every week, one of them posts a paper from the list. Each post starts with a personal reflection: how they found it, why it matters, and what it made them think. They tag the author and include the unique DOI, so that those who are interested can look up the paper.

What followed was a ripple effect. Researchers commented, shared, and tagged others. A community, named the Data Studies Bibliography (Aaltonen & Stelmaszak, 2024), began to take shape around the posts. A blog soon followed on the website where Aleksi and Marta discuss how they decide which papers go on the list, and a mailing list. Guest posts on the blog have brought in early career researcher voices.

According to Marta, they never post their own work: "Academics usually post about their own work. But in this community, we avoid it ourselves. It's not about me and my research but about the others", she says.

Looking back, Aleksi has come to the realisation that Marta and he have not "built" a community from their social media use. It was as if the community was already there but hidden: "A more accurate way of putting it is that we are making the community visible to itself".

For academics, this shift has significant implications. We believe that the platforms that will prove most valuable for scholars will be those that best support the interest graph, while maintaining the elements of the social graph that ensure your own sense of community and belonging. The COVID-19 pandemic foreshadowed this general trend, as social media offered an opportunity for information sharing, networking, and serendipitous encounters (see also Box 3.3) on the interest graph—precisely the kind of experiences that hitherto had taken place at in-person conferences and seminars (Bogers, 2021).

The migration away from X has accelerated a broader shift in how researchers approach social media. As our overview of the different platforms in Chapter 3 illustrates, we are witnessing several trends.

There is an increased specialisation in the use of platforms. Rather than one single "academic social media" platform, researchers are increasingly using different platforms for different purposes: LinkedIn for professional networking, Bluesky for informal scholarly discussion, ResearchGate for paper sharing, and so forth.

At the same time, there is an increased need for greater user control over feeds and content. In response to users' frustrations with algorithmically curated newsfeeds, many platforms now offer more fine-grained controls over what users see, moving away from "black box" recommendation algorithms.

There is also concern about the longevity of social media platforms. Some researchers—and perhaps especially more senior ones—are more hesitant about investing heavily in platforms that are new, might disappear, or radically change. This has led to a greater use of cross-posting tools as a kind of "diversification" strategy, and the interest in a more resilient fediverse (see Chapter 3), where one commercial platform will no longer have control over your entire history of posts.

Moreover, there is a rebalancing between open and closed spaces. While public platforms remain important for wide dissemination, there is renewed interest in more controlled environments like Discord servers, WhatsApp groups, and invitation-only forums for deeper conversations.

Finally, there is more attention to how to integrate social media with general research workflows. Social media tools are increasingly integrated with other aspects of the research process, from reference management to data visualisation to preprint sharing, which also has implications for their use and efficacy.

These trends reflect a more mature use of social media by academics. Researchers are moving beyond the initial excitement of social platforms to develop more intentional and strategic approaches based on their specific needs and goals.

Navigating tensions and trade-offs: A balancing act

In line with what we presented in Chapter 10 and the previous section, academic social media use inevitably involves navigating various tensions and trade-offs. Understanding these dynamics can help you make more informed choices about your social media practices. While the Researcher's Social Media Compass (Figure 10.1) helps you orient your social media strategy, Figure 11.1 illustrates the balancing act that follows. Each scale reflects a dynamic tension that scholars must continuously manage as they use social media.

Time investment vs. reward

Academic schedules are already crowded with research, teaching, and administrative responsibilities. Social media can easily consume whatever time you allow. While some researchers may hardly spend any time on social media, others may spend several hours per week, not only posting and interacting, but creating more elaborate content, moderating, discussing, and networking.

The relationship between the time you invest and your returns is rarely linear. Often, there are threshold effects, where a minimal level of consistent activity is necessary before networks begin to form and your posts gain "traction" on the platforms and visibility in terms of audience views. Beyond a certain point, diminishing returns set in as

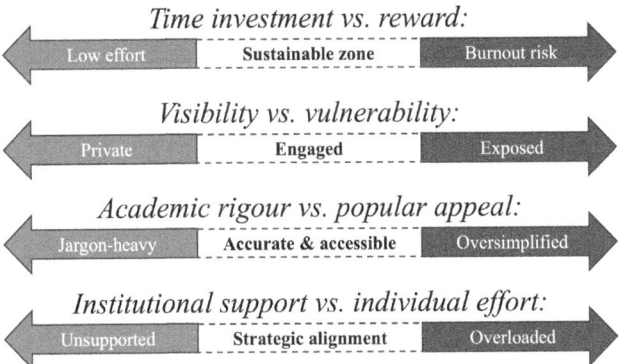

FIGURE 11.1   Navigating tensions in academic social media use.

additional time spent yields progressively smaller benefits. Long-term consistent work and interactions tend to produce compounding benefits, however, with accelerating returns as networks grow and your own archives of content build up.

Finding your optimal balance requires that you experiment and honestly assess the value you are receiving relative to your other professional activities. To this end, some scholars find it helpful to set specific time boundaries or batch social media activities into designated periods rather than allowing them to fragment attention throughout the workday.

Visibility vs. vulnerability

Greater visibility inevitably increases your vulnerability to criticism, misunderstanding, and various forms of online negativity. As we discussed in Chapter 8, this can range from reasonable scholarly disagreement to trolling and harassment.

The visibility-vulnerability dynamic creates particular challenges for early career researchers who benefit most from visibility but may lack institutional protection, for scholars from underrepresented groups who often face disproportionate criticism and harassment, for those working on politically sensitive topics where public attention can be intense and polarised, and for researchers whose findings challenge powerful interests in industry, government, or society.

Managing this tension requires both individual strategies (such as those outlined in Chapter 8) and institutional support (as also discussed in the previous section). Many academics develop a gradual approach to visibility, starting with more professional and scholarly audiences, before potentially widening their reach to broader audiences. Others collaborate with communications offices or more experienced colleagues when addressing sensitive topics. In general, we believe that while developing resilience to criticism is an important skill for academics, institutions should also actively protect vulnerable scholars.

Academic rigour vs. popular appeal

Translating complex scholarly ideas for broader audiences involves simplification. Yet, oversimplification can distort or misrepresent research, particularly in nuanced fields. This creates a tension between maintaining scientific accuracy and creating accessible posts that resonate with your readers and viewers.

Academics who successfully navigate this tension typically identify core concepts that can be communicated accurately without technical details. They use analogies and examples that preserve essential meaning, acknowledge limitations and uncertainties even in simplified explanations, direct interested audiences to more detailed resources, and recognise that different platforms and formats require different levels of detail. As such, using social media should align with your science communication approach, which will be more effective if you maintain a "ladder of complexity" in your content, allowing audiences to jump in at different levels of sophistication.

This tension often manifests itself when research receives media attention or goes viral, creating pressure to respond quickly at the expense of nuance (see Chapter 8). In order to be flexible when managing these situations, it may be useful to have prepared approaches for translating your work. You can, for example, develop "escalator pitches" (rather than "elevator pitches") in which your explanations start with accessible entry points, but that can be extended to incorporate more complexity as audience interest and understanding permit. This approach would allow you to interact with a wide range of audiences without sacrificing your intellectual integrity.

Institutional support vs. individual effort

Most universities now encourage researchers to actively seek out broader audiences, but institutional support for these activities varies widely. This can create a tension between your institution's expectations and the resources that are needed to meet them.

Few universities provide comprehensive training in digital communication or protected time for social media activities. Institutions may also often simultaneously encourage public outreach and interaction but discourage controversy or negative attention. University departments also rarely budget for social media training, communication tools, visual design support, or other resources that enhance the use of digital tools.

This problem is particularly pertinent to early and mid-career academics who have both the most to lose and the most to gain from sharing research and interacting with wider audiences. Navigating this tension requires clear communication with department chairs and administrators about expectations and resources—and how the use of social media aligns with institutional priorities.

Some academics successfully advocate for training, tools, and support for social media activity by framing them in terms of institutional priorities like research impact, student recruitment, or grant acquisition. You too should consider setting up networks of scholars within your institutions to collectively advocate for training, tools, and support, as institutional change is more likely to be produced by coordinated advocacy efforts than by isolated individual requests.

Closing this book, opening new paths

We started this book with a quiet moment—a doctor on a sofa, puzzling over a clinical question. What followed for him wasn't a paper or a proposal, but a thread on a social media platform—one that triggered a discussion, brought fresh attention to a long-standing problem, and ultimately led to a new study. It's a reminder that research impact often begins outside formal academic channels, in small, visible acts of curiosity. We believe social media have a role to play within science, and in how science connects with society. Across the chapters, we've seen how researchers use these platforms not only to broadcast results but to meet collaborators, test ideas, work with others, and make sense of what their research means in public. Impact, in this light, isn't a fixed path from question to outcome. It's a horizon shaped by weak ties, chance interactions, and careful choices.

This book ends here, but the work of bringing research into conversation with the world is open—not finished. Our world faces complex challenges that need researchers who are open-minded and eager to make a real difference. If you've read this far, dear reader, the chances are you're one of them.

For you, as an individual researcher, social media can be a pathway to professional growth. Social media might not define how you do your research, but how you use them can shape who your research reaches, how you develop, and what kind of researcher you become in the process.

As you close this book, we hope you've also opened up—to embracing social media for research impact.

REFERENCES

Aaltonen, A., & Stelmaszak, M. (2024). DataStudiesBibliography.org. *SSRN Electronic Journal.* http://dx.doi.org/10.2139/ssrn.4765456

Afuah, A. (2013). Are network effects really all about size? The role of structure and conduct. *Strategic Management Journal, 34*(3), 257–273. https://doi.org/10.1002/smj.2013

Albris, K., Fast, K., Karlsen, F., Kaun, A., Lomborg, S., & Syvertsen, T. (Eds.). (2024). *The digital backlash and the paradoxes of disconnection.* University of Gothenburg.

Andreasen, J. R. (2025), When climate research fuels climate myths: Author insights from a misused publication. *Eos*, 106. https://doi.org/10.1029/2025EO250034

Audrezet, A., de Kerviler, G., & Guidry Moulard, J. (2020). Authenticity under threat: When social media influencers need to go beyond self-presentation. *Journal of Business Research, 117*, 557–569. https://doi.org/10.1016/j.jbusres.2018.10.008

Bastow, S., Dunleavy, P., & Tinkler, J. (2014). *The impact of the social sciences: How academics and their research make a difference.* Sage.

Beck, S., Bergenholtz, C., Bogers, M., Brasseur, T.-M., Conradsen, M. L., Di Marco, D., Distel, A. P., Dobusch, L., Dörler, D., Effert, A., Fecher, B., Filiou, D., Frederiksen, L., Gillier, T., Grimpe, C., Gruber, M., Haeussler, C., Heigl, F., Hoisl, K., Hyslop, K., Kokshagina, O., LaFlamme, M., Lawson, C., Lifshitz-Assaf, H., Lukas, W., Nordberg, M., Norn, M. T., Poetz, M., Ponti, M., Pruschak, G., Pujol Priego, L., Radziwon, A., Rafner, J., Romanova, G., Ruser, A., Sauermann, H., Shah, S. K., Sherson, J. F., Suess-Reyes, J., Tucci, C. L., Tuertscher, P., Vedel, J. B., Velden, T., Verganti, R., Wareham, J., Wiggins, A., & Xu, S. M. (2022). The Open Innovation in Science research field: A collaborative conceptualisation approach. *Industry and Innovation, 29*(2), 136–185. https://doi.org/10.1080/13662716.2020.1792274

Binder, M. (2024, February 16). The majority of traffic from Elon Musk's X may have been fake during the Super Bowl, report suggests. *Mashable.* https://mashable.com/article/x-twitter-elon -musk-bots-fake-traffic

Bogers, M. (2021). Five principles for scientists on social media. *Nature, 593*(7857), 37. https://doi.org/10.1038/d41586-021-01294-3

Bogers, M., Zobel, A.-K., Afuah, A., Almirall, E., Brunswicker, S., Dahlander, L., Frederiksen, L., Gawer, A., Gruber, M., Haefliger, S., Hagedoorn, J., Hilgers, D., Laursen, K., Magnusson, M. G., Majchrzak, A., McCarthy, I. P., Moeslein, K. M., Nambisan, S., Piller, F. T., Radziwon, A., Rossi-Lamastra, C., Sims, J., & Ter Wal, A. L. J. (2017). The open innovation research landscape: Established perspectives and emerging themes across different levels of analysis. *Industry and Innovation, 24*(1), 8–40. https://doi.org/10.1080 /13662716.2016.1240068

Bonacchi, C., Krzyzanska, M., & Acerbi, A. (2025). Positive sentiment and expertise predict the diffusion of archaeological content on social media. *Scientific Reports, 15,* 2031. https://doi.org/10.1038 /s41598-025-85167-z

Borkin, M. A., Vo, A. A., Bylinskii, Z., Isola, P., Sunkavalli, S., Oliva, A., & Pfister, H. (2013). What makes a visualization memorable? *IEEE Transactions on Visualization and Computer Graphics, 19*(12), 2306–2315. https://doi.org/10.1109/TVCG.2013.234

Bornmann, L. (2014). Do altmetrics point to the broader impact of research? An overview of benefits and disadvantages of altmetrics. *Journal of Informetrics, 8*(4), 895–903. https://doi.org/10.1016/j.joi .2014.09.005

Busch, C. (2024). Towards a theory of serendipity: A systematic review and conceptualization. *Journal of Management Studies, 61*(3), 1110–1151. https://doi.org/10.1111/joms.12890

Carrigan, M. (2019). *Social media for academics* (2nd ed.). Sage.

Chandler, D., & Munday, R. (2016). Social media. In D. Chandler & R. Munday (Eds.), *A dictionary of social media.* Oxford University Press.

Chesbrough, H., & Bogers, M. (2014). Explicating open innovation: Clarifying an emerging paradigm for understanding innovation. In H. Chesbrough, W. Vanhaverbeke, & J. West (Eds.), *New frontiers in open innovation* (pp. 3–28). Oxford University Press. https://doi .org/10.1093/acprof:oso/9780199682461.003.0001

Costa, C. (2013). The habitus of digital scholars. *Research in Learning Technology, 21,* 21274. https://doi.org/10.3402/rlt.v21i0.21274

Etzkowitz, H., Webster, A., Gebhardt, C., & Terra, B. R. C. (2000). The future of the university and the university of the future: Evolution of ivory tower to entrepreneurial paradigm. *Research Policy, 29*(2), 313–330. https://doi.org/10.1016/S0048-7333(99)00069-4

European Commission. (2025). *EU valorisation policy: Making research results work for society.* https://research-and-innovation .ec.europa.eu/research-area/industrial-research-and-innovation/eu -valorisation-policy_en

Fecher, B., Friesike, S. (2014). Open science: One term, five schools of thought. In S. Bartling & S. Friesike. (Eds.), *Opening science* (pp. 17–47). Springer. https://doi.org/10.1007/978-3-319-00026-8_2

Fransman, J. (2013). Researching academic literacy practices around Twitter: Performative methods and their onto-ethical implications. In R. Goodfellow & M. Lea (Eds.), *Literacy in the digital university: Critical perspectives on learning, scholarship, and technology* (pp. 27–41). Routledge.

Gosse, C., Veletsianos, G., Hodson, J., Houlden, S., Dousay, T. A., Lowenthal, P. R., & Hall, N. (2021). The hidden costs of connectivity: Nature and effects of scholars' online harassment. *Learning, Media and Technology, 46*(3), 264–280. https://doi.org/10.1080/17439884.2021.1878218

Granovetter, M. S. (1973). The strength of weak ties. *American Journal of Sociology, 78*(6), 1360–1380. https://doi.org/10.1086/225469

Grant, A. (2013). *Give and take: Why helping others drives our success.* Viking.

Greenhow, C., & Gleason, B. (2014). Social scholarship: Reconsidering scholarly practices in the age of social media. *British Journal of Educational Technology, 45*(3), 392–402. https://doi.org/10.1111/bjet.12150

Guerrero, M., & Urbano, D. (2012). The development of an entrepreneurial university. *Journal of Technology Transfer, 37*, 43–74. https://doi.org/10.1007/s10961-010-9171-x

Haimson, O. L., Liu, T., Zhang, B. Z., & Corvite, S. (2021). The online authenticity paradox: What being "authentic" on social media means, and barriers to achieving it. *Proceedings of the ACM on Human-Computer Interaction, 5*(CSCW2), 1–18. https://doi.org/10.1145/3479564

Harzing, A. W., & Alakangas, S. (2016). Google scholar, scopus and the web of science: A longitudinal and cross-disciplinary comparison. *Scientometrics, 106*(2), 787–804. https://doi.org/10.1007/s11192-015-1798-9

Hirsch, J. E. (2005). An index to quantify an individual's scientific research output. *Proceedings of the National Academy of Sciences, 102*(46), 16569–16572. https://doi.org/10.1073/pnas.0507655102

Hoffman, A. J. (2021). *The engaged scholar: Expanding the impact of academic research in today's world.* Stanford University Press.

Holgersson, M., Dahlander, L., Chesbrough, H., & Bogers, M. L. A. M. (2024). Open Innovation in the Age of AI. *California Management Review, 67*(1), 5–20. https://doi.org/10.1177/00081256241279326

Håhr Jensen, L. (2022, June 22). *How to handle critics on social media.* Workshop for community managers, NUAS Communication Conference, Turku.

IMDB. (2025). Pay it forward. Retrieved January 4, 2025, from https://www.imdb.com/title/tt0223897/

Katz, E., Blumler, J. G., & Gurevitch, M. (1973). Uses and gratifications research. *The Public Opinion Quarterly*, *37*(4), 509–523. https://doi.org/10.1086/268109

Kietzmann, J. H., Hermkens, K., McCarthy, I. P., & Silvestre, B. S. (2011). Social media? Get serious! Understanding the functional building blocks of social media. *Business Horizons*, *54*(3), 241–251. https://doi.org/10.1016/j.bushor.2011.01.005

Kjellberg, S. (2014). Researchers' blogging practices in two epistemic cultures: The scholarly blog as a situated genre. *Human IT*, *12*(3), 36–77. http://etjanst.hb.se/bhs/ith/3-12/sk.htm

Klofsten, M., Brem, A., Guerrero, M., & Urbano, D. (2024). Intrapreneurial universities in digital times: New ways of thinking and future challenges. *Technovation*, *135*, 103069. https://doi.org/10.1016/j.technovation.2023.103069

Klofsten, M., Fayolle, A., Guerrero, M., Mian, S., Urbano, D., & Wright, M. (2019). The entrepreneurial university as a driver for economic growth and social change: Key strategic challenges. *Technological Forecasting and Social Change*, *141*, 149–158. https://doi.org/10.1016/j.techfore.2018.12.004

Koshin, S. A. (2024). Shamed into silence online: The sexualized, personal hate reserved for Somali women. *The Guardian*. https://www.theguardian.com/global-development/2024/dec/04/somali-women-online-social-media-online-hate-speech-abuse

Leonardi, P. M. (2014). Social media, knowledge sharing, and innovation: Toward a theory of communication visibility. *Information Systems Research*, *25*(4), 796–816. https://doi.org/10.1287/isre.2014.0536

Lin, N. (2001). *Social capital: A theory of social structure and action.* Cambridge University Press.

Liu, W. (2017). The changing role of non-English papers in scholarly communication: Evidence from Web of Science's three journal citation indexes. *Learned Publishing*, *30*(2), 115–123. https://doi.org/10.1002/leap.1089

Lorentzen, M. K., Dall, N., & Thielke, K. M. (2019). *Kan trold tæmmes? Trolling og debatkultur i den digitale tidsalder*. Informations Forlag. (Book in Danish. English translation of title: Can the troll be tamed? Trolling and debate culture in the digital age.)

Luc, J. G. Y., Archer, M. A., Arora, R. C., Bender, E. M., Blitz, A., Cooke, D. T., & Antonoff, M. B. (2021). Does tweeting improve citations? One-year results from the TSSMN prospective randomized trial. *The Annals of Thoracic Surgery*, *111*(1), 296–300. https://doi.org/10.1016/j.athoracsur.2020.04.065

Marwick, A. E., & boyd, d. (2011). I tweet honestly, I tweet passionately: Twitter users, context collapse, and the imagined audience. *New Media & Society*, *13*(1), 114–133. https://doi.org/10.1177/1461444810365313

McCarthy, I. P., & Bogers, M. L. A. M. (2023). The open academic: Why and how business academics should use social media to be more 'open' and impactful. *Business Horizons*, 66(1), 153–166. https://doi.org/10.1016/j.bushor.2022.05.001

Mollick, E. R., & Mollick, L. (2022). New modes of learning enabled by AI chatbots: Three methods and assignments. *SSRN Electronic Journal*. https://ssrn.com/abstract=4300783

Mowery, D. C., Nelson, R. R., Sampat, B. N., & Ziedonis, A. A. (2004). *Ivory tower and industrial innovation: University-industry technology transfer before and after the Bayh-Dole Act*. Stanford University Press.

Newport, C. (2016). *Deep work: Rules for focused success in a distracted world*. Grand Central Publishing.

Olson, R. (2018). *Houston, we have a narrative: Why science needs story*. University of Chicago Press.

Podsakoff, N. P., Whiting, S. W., Podsakoff, P. M., & Blume, B. D. (2009). Individual- and organizational-level consequences of organizational citizenship behaviors: A meta-analysis. *Journal of Applied Psychology*, 94(1), 122–141. https://doi.org/10.1037/a0013079

Priem, J., Taraborelli, D., Groth, P., & Neylon, C. (2010). Altmetrics: A manifesto. http://altmetrics.org/manifesto/

Rao, V. (2019). Venkatesh Rao on Waldenponding. Econtalk podcast with host Russ Roberts. https://www.econtalk.org/venkatesh-rao-on-waldenponding/

Rapoport, A. (1953). Spread of information through a population with socio-structural bias: I. Assumption of transitivity. *Bulletin of Mathematical Biophysics*, 15, 523–533. https://doi.org/10.1007/BF02476440

Roos, G., Olavarria-Contreras, G., Luirink, M., Moreira, J. J. S., Groeneveld, L. F., Haak, W., & Weiner, A. (2020). Online conferences–Towards a new (virtual) reality. *Computational and Theoretical Chemistry*, 1189, 112975. https://doi.org/10.1016/j.comptc.2020.112975

Sharma, G., & Bansal, P. (2023). Partnering up: Including managers as research partners in systematic reviews. *Organizational Research Methods*, 26(2), 262–291. https://doi.org/10.1177/10944281211066677

Trifiro, B. M., & Gerson, J. (2019). Social media usage patterns: Research note on the development and validation of the Social Media Engagement Scale (SMES). *Communication Research Reports*, 36(1), 54–60. https://doi.org/10.1080/08824096.2018.1542769

Van de Ven, A. H. (2007). *Engaged scholarship: A guide for organizational and social research*. Oxford University Press.

Veletsianos, G., Houlden, S., Hodson, J., & Gosse, C. (2018). Women scholars' experiences with online harassment and abuse: Self-protection, resistance, acceptance, and self-blame. *New Media & Society*, 20(12), 4689–4708. https://doi.org/10.1177/1461444818781324

Veletsianos, G., & Kimmons, R. (2012). Networked participatory scholarship: Emergent techno-cultural pressures toward open and digital scholarship in online networks. *Computers & Education*, *58*(2), 766–774. https://doi.org/10.1016/j.compedu.2011.10.001

Verduyn, P., Ybarra, O., Résibois, M., Jonides, J., & Kross, E. (2017). Do social network sites enhance or undermine subjective well-being? A critical review. *Social Issues and Policy Review*, *11*(1), 274–302. https://doi.org/10.1111/sipr.12033

Voytek, B. (2017). Social media, open science, and data science are inextricably linked. *Neuron*, *96*(6), 1219–1222. https://doi.org/10.1016/j.neuron.2017.11.015

VSNU, NFU, KNAW, NWO, & ZonMw. (2019). *Room for everyone's talent: Towards a new balance in the recognition and rewards of academics*. https://www.nwo.nl/sites/nwo/files/media-files/2019-Recognition-Rewards-Position-Paper_EN.pdf

Wang, X., Koneru, S., & Rajtmajer, S. (2024). The failed migration of academic Twitter. *arXiv preprint*. https://doi.org/10.48550/arXiv.2406.04005

Weller, M. (2011). *The digital scholar: How technology is transforming scholarly practice*. Bloomsbury Academic.

Young, M. (2018). The strength of weak ties: Why researchers use Twitter and LinkedIn. https://mikeyoungacademy.dk/the-strength-of-weak-ties/

Young, M. (2024a). Bluesky is emerging as the new platform for science. https://mikeyoungacademy.dk/bluesky-is-emerging-as-the-new-platform-for-science/

Young, M. (2024b). Ethics part 2: Why do scientists use social media? https://mikeyoungacademy.dk/ethics-part-2-why-do-scientists-use-social-media/

Zak, P. J. (2017). The neuroscience of trust. *Harvard Business Review*, *95*(1), 84–90. https://hbr.org/2017/01/the-neuroscience-of-trust

Zhang, B., & Lu, Y. (2023). Are scientists credible social media influencers? Perceived authority and persuasion in science communication. *Public Understanding of Science*, *32*(6), 670–685. https://doi.org/10.1177/09636625231157402

Zuboff, S. (2019). *The age of surveillance capitalism: The fight for a human future at the new frontier of power*. PublicAffairs.

INDEX

Note: Page numbers in **bold** reference tables.

For Product Safety Concerns and Information please contact our
EU representative GPSR@taylorandfrancis.com Taylor & Francis
Verlag GmbH, Kaufingerstraße 24, 80331 München, Germany